THE JEWISH QUARTERLY

The Jewish Quarterly is published four times a year
by The Jewish Quarterly Pty Ltd
Publisher: Morry Schwartz

ISBN 9781922517104 E-ISBN 9781743822302
ISSN 0449010X E-ISSN 23262516

Essays, reviews and correspondence © retained by the authors
Photograph of Rose Herzig supplied by Rachel Kadish; photograph of
Hotel Kryniczanka from the Polish National Digital Archives; photograph
of Zuzanna Ginczanka: Adam Mickiewicz Museum of Literature,
Warsaw via Wikimedia Commons

Subscriptions 1 year print & digital (4 issues): £42 GBP | $56 USD.
1 year digital only: £25 GBP | $32 USD. Payment may be made
by Mastercard or Visa. Payment includes postage and handling.

Subscribe online at jewishquarterly.com or email subscribe@jewishquarterly.com
Correspondence should be addressed to: The Editor, The Jewish Quarterly,
22–24 Northumberland Street, Collingwood VIC 3066 Australia
Phone +61 3 9486 0288 Email enquiries@jewishquarterly.com

The Jewish Quarterly is published under licence from the
Jewish Literary Trust Limited, which exercises a governance function.

UK Company Number: 01189861. UK Charity Commission Number: 268589.

Issue 247, February 2022

THE JEWISH QUARTERLY

Contributors

Benjamin Balint, author of *Kafka's Last Trial*, is writing a book about the Polish-Jewish artist and writer Bruno Schulz.

Eva Hoffman grew up in Kraków and has written widely on emigration and exile, including the book *After Such Knowledge: Reflections on the Long Aftermath of the Holocaust.*

Rachel Kadish's most recent novel, *The Weight of Ink*, received a National Jewish Book Award. She lives outside Boston.

Menachem Kaiser is a writer living in Brooklyn, New York. He is the author of *Plunder: A Memoir of Family Property and Nazi Treasure.*

Tali Lavi is a critic, writer and public interviewer, and a programmer for Melbourne Jewish Book Week.

Benjamin Ramm is a writer and broadcaster living in Nice, France.

Lior Sternfeld is Associate Professor of History and Jewish Studies at Penn State University and author of *Between Iran and Zion: Jewish Histories of Twentieth-Century Iran.*

Paper brigade

The incredible story of the Vilnius archive

Menachem Kaiser

Perhaps the most significant Jewish archive in Eastern Europe before World War II was that of YIVO, the *Yidisher Visnshaftlekher Institut* (Yiddish Scientific Institute), in Vilnius, then part of Poland. Not due to its size – though it was considerable, with nearly 80,000 items, plus 40,000 books – but to its subject, which was, simply and elusively, the daily lives of Eastern European Jews. YIVO, established in 1925, had a broad mandate – it was a leading educational and cultural institution, with departments for research, pedagogy, philology and history, but its founding premise was that all aspects of Jewish life ought to be rigorously, scientifically studied. Even – or especially – quotidian objects and documents, from synagogue records to lullabies, were considered significant. One of YIVO's most successful and emblematic initiatives was the *zamler* programme, which deputised laypeople in hundreds of cities across Poland and beyond to collect folklore; YIVO was soon deluged with tens of thousands of items. This was in addition to 10,000 newspaper issues; hundreds of youth memoirs; thousands of pages related to pogroms, including eyewitness accounts;

rare manuscripts; correspondence and journals from some of the most notable people of the nineteenth and twentieth centuries; photographs; groundbreaking Yiddish bibliographic material; pamphlets; and posters. In aggregate, the archive offered a portrait, simultaneously expansive and granular, of a world about to be wiped out.

The Nazis occupied Vilnius on 24 June 1941; within weeks, the *Einsatzstab Reichsleiter Rosenberg* (ERR), the agency charged with assessing and appropriating cultural property, ransacked YIVO and other museums, archives and libraries, carting off the most valuable books, incunabula (books published before 1501) and manuscripts. For the next eight months, the modern and spacious YIVO building was used as a barracks for a unit of the Luftwaffe; thousands of documents and books were haphazardly damaged or destroyed. Organised looting resumed in April 1942 under the leadership of Johannes Pohl, a Hebrew-speaking Old Testament scholar and former priest who was the ERR's Hebraica expert and the chief librarian of the Institute for Research on the Jewish Question in Frankfurt. Pohl ordered a select portion of YIVO's collection to be sent to Frankfurt, a task that required knowledgeable, literate workers. A team was recruited from the Vilna Ghetto. The ERR had already requisitioned Herman Kruk, head of the ghetto library; Zelig Kalmanovich, director of YIVO; and Chaikl Lunksi, director of the Strashun library, a beloved public lending library that was being similarly plundered; and they in turn hired a team of twenty, mostly writers and intellectuals, including Abraham Sutzkever, one of the greatest Yiddish poets of the twentieth century, and Shmerke Kaczerginski, a poet and musician who wrote or collected the majority of Holocaust songs known to us today. Within the ghetto this group became known, with a touch of derision, as the paper brigade – the YIVO building was outside the ghetto and considered a desirable worksite, with fairly lax German oversight and relatively light labour.

But it was heartbreaking work. The members of the paper brigade were only too aware of the value of what they were being forced to give to the Nazis or destroy. A maximum of 30 per cent of the material was to be sent to Frankfurt, with the remainder marked for the mill.

They sought to preserve what they could, though there was a debate over the best course of action. Kalmanovich believed the most valuable items should be sent to Frankfurt, where they would be properly stored and, hopefully, survive the war. But he was in the minority, and the others launched an extensive and sustained smuggling operation. Books and documents were transported out of YIVO

> *Many in the ghetto thought it lunacy to take such a risk for something inedible*

and into the ghetto, and placed in crates in specially constructed *malinas*, or hiding spots, often in cooperation with the Fareynikte Partizaner Organizatsye (FPO), the ghetto's underground partisan organisation. The largest *malina*, at 6 Shavel Street, descended more than 18 metres underground, had its own ventilation system and siphoned electricity from outside the ghetto.

Thousands of books and hundreds of thousands of documents, from YIVO and many other institutions, were hidden in the ghetto. Kruk, who had a permit that allowed him to enter and exit the ghetto without being searched, was a particularly enthusiastic and capable smuggler. Others would stuff papers inside their clothing, or use a wagon with a false bottom, or employ any number of creative tactics. Sutzkever once obtained authorisation to bring "wastepaper" – in fact letters by Tolstoy, Gorky, Bialik and Sholem Aleichem – into the ghetto to be used as fuel. Occasionally they were caught with the literary contraband and severely beaten. (Smuggling paper wasn't as serious an offence as smuggling food, but even so, many in the ghetto thought it lunacy to take such a risk for something inedible.) Later they created hiding spots in the attic and basement of the YIVO building, secreting as many as 5000 books onsite. Material was also given to sympathetic Lithuanians, most notably Ona Šimaitė, a librarian at Vilnius University.

The sorting – and the smuggling – ceased in August 1943, a few weeks before the ghetto was liquidated. Members of the paper brigade who were part of the FPO, including Kaczerginski and Sutzkever, escaped to the forest. Most of the others were killed.

The Soviets liberated Vilnius in July 1944; within days, Kaczerginski, Sutzkever and other partisans began to retrieve the hidden material. The YIVO building was a pile of rubble, and most of the *malinas* had been destroyed or were unreachable. But at least three were intact and accessible, including the bunker at 6 Shavel Street – which contained nearly thirty crates. Initially they stored the material in Kaczerginski's apartment, and then – somehow securing approval from the communist authorities – they succeeded in establishing a Jewish museum, housed in the former ghetto library. By 1945, the museum held 25,000 books and tens of thousands of documents.

The material that had been sent to Frankfurt, from YIVO as well as from hundreds of other Jewish institutions across Europe, was discovered soon after the war in cellars of bombed-out buildings, in caves, castles, schools, barns and offices. It amounted to the largest Judaica collection in history. American forces stored and processed the material in a depot in Offenbach, outside Frankfurt. More than 75,000 items were identified as YIVO's.

YIVO had survived as an institution, even as its building in Vilnius had been destroyed. Max Weinreich, a founder and director, had been en route to Denmark for a linguistics conference when the war broke out; he never returned to Vilnius, and in 1940 moved to New York, where he re-established YIVO's American branch as the new headquarters.

Weinreich was desperate to secure YIVO's material and have it sent to New York, but the process was enormously fraught and complex. Standard restitution practice was to send material to its country of origin, and anything defined as heirless Jewish property was given to Jewish Cultural Reconstruction (JCR), a consortium of trustee organisations that distributed it to Jewish communities around the world. The YIVO material was being claimed by the Soviets – with support from the Jewish Museum in Vilnius – as well as by JCR, and the US War Department and State Department issued conflicting orders. Weinreich, however, proved adept at navigating bureaucracies and currying favour with American officials, particularly those who had ties to Vilnius and/or YIVO. He successfully lobbied to have YIVO New York recognised as a valid American institution and a successor organisation to YIVO Vilna. And worsening US–Soviet relations meant that the United States did not formally recognise the Soviets' annexation of the Baltic states, and would not restitute material there. Finally, on 21 June 1947, the Americans – acting unliterally, without approval from their Allied partners – shipped 420 crates containing 79,204 items. The crates were initially housed in a Manischewitz company warehouse in New Jersey before being sent on to YIVO. Over the next five years, nearly 12,000 additional items were sent from Offenbach to YIVO.

It's a triumphant story of reclamation, but also more than that – because not everything that was sent to YIVO had belonged to YIVO before the war. Nearly three-quarters of the more than 34,000 books were originally from the Strashun library, and at least some of the archival material had belonged to other, no longer extant, institutions; the crates had been marked "YIVO & Associated Libraries". Over the years, YIVO has offered shifting explanations as to how the Strashun library books became the property of YIVO – Strashun trustees had asked YIVO to ship their books to safety; the Nazis had merged the two libraries; the Strashun books had been physically taken to the YIVO building – but none are supported by documentary evidence. The consensus among historians is that Weinreich, along with other representatives and allies of YIVO, may have stretched the truth in order to have non-YIVO material from Vilnius, most notably from the Strashun library, recognised as YIVO's and sent to New York.

This is not a condemnation of YIVO – not of its means nor its ends; there is a fine line, sometimes, between theft and salvation. What YIVO did was a response to the chaos, the obliteration, unleashed by the Nazis; it was a desperate, if indiscriminate, gathering of what had survived and what was now, again, in danger – the Soviets successfully claimed more than 1000 crates from Offenbach, much of which disappeared into the Soviet void. Almost by default, YIVO, as the only Jewish institution from Vilnius to have survived the war, became the bearer of the memory of Vilnius Jewry.

It was a role that was reinforced when YIVO began receiving items that had been smuggled out of the Jewish Museum in Vilnius – first by Sutzkever, and later, once the Soviets' antagonism towards Jewish memory and culture became overwhelmingly clear, by Kaczerginski. The two of them smuggled thousands of documents – including an eighteenth-century record book of the Vilna Gaon's synagogue and diaries written in the ghetto – through Poland and then Paris and finally to YIVO, where they became the Sutzkever-Kaczerginski collection, one of YIVO's core holdings.

Soviet authorities shut down the Jewish Museum in 1949, divvying up its material between several state-run institutions. In subsequent years, anti-Jewish sentiment in the Soviet Union intensified, and Hebrew and Yiddish books were destroyed en masse by institutions and individuals. From the other side of the Iron Curtain, it seemed all but certain that the books and documents that remained in Vilnius, despite surviving the Nazis, were now gone.

*

In April 1988, Sam Norich, then the executive director of YIVO, travelled to Poland for a photo exhibition. A couple of days before his flight home, he received a cryptic message from one of YIVO's researchers, Lucjan Dobroszycki, that a meeting had been arranged in Warsaw at the home of a local historian. Norich wasn't informed of the meeting's purpose, nor who would be there, but it was made clear that Norich would be interested to hear whatever it was that whoever this was had to say.

So Norich went to the home of the historian, and met the man who had orchestrated the meeting: a thirty-year-old Jewish Lithuanian named Emanuelis Zingeris. Zingeris was a university lecturer who had written his dissertation on Jewish cultural heritage in Lithuania. He was also a rising star in Sajūdis, the political organisation leading the struggle for Lithuanian independence – hence the secrecy: Zingeris was almost certainly being tracked by Soviet authorities. Zingeris had gone to all this trouble in order to tell Norich that, in the course of his graduate research, he had spent time in the Book Chamber, a state-run book storage facility housed in a former monastery, and had come across books and documents that were clearly YIVO's. But he offered few details, wouldn't specify which books or documents, how many there were, or what condition they were in. He said only that when the time was right, he'd be in touch. There was nothing Norich could do but go back to New York and wait.

"Zingeris," Norich told me, "was baiting the hook."

A few months later, Zingeris got in touch, and invited Norich to come to Vilnius, officially in order to attend the founding meeting of the Jewish Culture Society. Norich readily accepted, and he and Marek Web, YIVO's chief archivist, made the trip in January 1989. The day after the meeting – at which, Norich says, Zingeris's political ambitions and talents were on full display – Zingeris brought Norich and Web to the Book Chamber. They took in the faded magnificence of the former monastery, the books stacked nearly to the ceiling. They met the director, who, after some small talk, had an employee wheel out a dolly on which were stacked five packages wrapped in brown paper and secured with twine.

The director selected a package and unwrapped it, revealing a stack of documents, which he passed, one at a time, to Norich and Web. Web – a Polish native, fluent in half a dozen languages and intimately familiar with YIVO's archive – immediately recognised many of these documents. He knew which collection they belonged to, the gaps they filled in. There were even letters, Norich told me, that responded to ones held in the New York archive. Each of the packages was similarly filled with documents, thousands in total, and this was, Zingeris intimated, only the tip of the iceberg. Afterwards, the packages were rewrapped and retied, stacked on the dolly and wheeled away.

*

Much of the material thought for forty years to have been lost or destroyed had in fact survived. When the Jewish Museum was dissolved in 1949, its holdings were inherited by the Book Chamber in Soviet-occupied Lithuania, and its director, Antanas Ulpis, a true bibliophile, safeguarded the books and documents, at considerable risk. Ulpis even persuaded Vilnius University to give him 10,000 Hebrew and Yiddish books it had planned to pulp, and secured from the Historical Revolutionary Museum and Institute for the History of the Communist Party their Jewish documents, which included parts of the Jewish Museum's archive. Many of the books he hid in plain sight, among the million-plus volumes stored in the monastery; he even clandestinely catalogued nearly 20,000 books with the help of Jewish bibliographers and volunteer pensioners. Ulpis wasn't authorised to store archives, let alone Jewish archives, but did

"It was clear that the archive had survived only because it had been hidden"

so anyway, burying them behind or underneath piles of books, in the basement – even inside an organ. He stored portions of the documents in different institutions, including the Library of the Academy of Sciences and the manuscript department of Lithuania's National Library.

Ulpis died in 1981 and left no account of his heroic act; his son, Dainius, told me that Ulpis never even told his wife what he had done. What we know we know from his staff, most of whom Ulpis never confided in, but who nonetheless picked up hints, or saw something unusual, or, later, discovered the material. In an interview, one employee, recorded as E.R., recounts moving a large pile of Soviet newspapers and finding 173 boxes of "Jewish material".

"Their physical state was terrible," E.R. said. "Crumpled, dirty pages; many of them torn, mouldy and wet. It was clear that the archive had survived only because it had been hidden."

*

Upon exiting the Book Chamber, Norich, beside himself, grabbed Zingeris's arm and told him that these documents belong to YIVO, and must be returned to YIVO. "I could see the smile fade from his face," Norich told me. "He turned away and said, 'We'll talk. It's not so easy.' I knew at that instant that Zingeris was going to be our chief proponent until he became our chief opponent."

Over the next few months, Norich attempted to persuade various Lithuanian officials to return the documents, or at least open a negotiation. But it was a turbulent time in Lithuania: the country was fitfully emerging from under Soviet rule, everything was in flux. One of the top Sajūdis officials agreed to return the material, Norich said, but was later deposed. Norich met twice with Vytautas Landsbergis, the chairman of Lithuania's Supreme Council (the highest-ranking official in those years), and once, in a motel in New Jersey, with future president Algirdas Brazauskas. But nothing came of it.

Zingeris, elected to parliament in 1990, was deeply involved; he was, according to Norich, "the only one [among Lithuanian politicians] to deal with Jewish matters; that was his brief". (Zingeris, who remains a member of parliament, initially agreed to be interviewed for this story but did not respond to numerous follow-up calls and messages.) Zingeris had helped found a Jewish museum in 1989 – later to be known as the Vilna Gaon Jewish State Museum – and he made it clear that he considered the material to be Lithuanian cultural heritage, and thus Lithuania's property. But he left open the possibility that something could be worked out.

The material was, clearly, a source of leverage. For Lithuania, newly independent, fighting for international recognition and standing, the material, Norich said, "meant an opening to America, meant money, meant the ability to influence Washington". At one point, a politician floated the idea of YIVO returning to Vilnius, or at least opening a branch there – Lithuanian officials had, of their own accord, already contacted a Finnish firm to design a new building, to be paid for by YIVO.

Norich eventually secured an agreement with the directors of the Lithuanian Central State Archives, which now housed most of the material. YIVO would provide microfilm equipment and archival training, and in exchange Lithuania would *lend* the material to YIVO, so it could be copied, catalogued and returned.

The Lithuanians reneged. Norich subsequently learned that the directors were excoriated by politicians for agreeing to a deal when it was clear that more could be squeezed out of the Americans. The deal was renegotiated – YIVO sweetened their offer, added more equipment. The Lithuanians signed, then reneged again.

In 1992, Norich was fired, Sajūdis lost the election, any ongoing negotiations were scrambled. A few years later, though, the new research director of YIVO, Allan Nadler, was able to secure a deal. Three crates were to be sent to YIVO to be catalogued and photocopied, then returned. But when the first two arrived, it seems YIVO's leadership seriously contemplated violating the agreement and keeping the documents. (A contemporaneous scholarly account concludes, triumphantly, that the "materials were shipped to YIVO … at long last reunited with their spiritual home and with the Jewish people".) It was a brewing scandal, with accusations and counter-accusations, but eventually YIVO relented and sent the two crates back. The third crate was never sent.

Over the next few years, the issue receded and the material stayed put, mostly unused, unseen, much of it improperly stored or misplaced. Fira Bramson, a devoted and talented Jewish Lithuanian librarian, did some preliminary cataloguing, but there were otherwise few people in the country interested in this material, or even able to read it. Every few years, maybe, a foreign scholar would come to Vilnius and pull up some documents. Jack Jacobs, a Fulbright scholar in Vilnius in 2009, described to me the experience of reading some of the pre-war Yiddish newspapers, how delicately he'd handle the pages and how, even then, they would disintegrate in his fingers.

By the time Jonathan Brent, the current director of YIVO, came on board in 2009, it was more or less a dead issue. Once a year, he told me, the Lithuanian foreign minister would visit and make the case that YIVO should relocate to Vilnius, but there was otherwise no substantive communication between YIVO and Lithuanian authorities.

*

YIVO's claim on the material in Lithuania, on the books and documents saved by Antanas Ulpis, is in fact tiered. There's the material that unquestionably belonged to YIVO before the war – books with a YIVO ex libris, for example, or documents clearly part of its archive. To this portion, a commonsense argument applies: what belonged to YIVO then should belong to YIVO now (given that YIVO New York is the successor organisation to YIVO Vilna). But a significant fraction of the material did not belong to YIVO before the war, or at best has uncertain provenance. (YIVO claims that nearly all of this non-YIVO material, which originated from a wide variety of Vilnius institutions, was given to it before the war, but in many cases there is no documentation to support this.) Then there's the material that was written during or after the war. In these instances YIVO, of course, has no obvious legal claim, but still there is, symbolically, narratively, an entanglement. Most (though not all) of the corresponding parts of these collections, or at least what's extant, is held in YIVO's New York archives – this is the material that was retrieved from Offenbach or smuggled out of the Jewish Museum.

Rightly or wrongly, YIVO became and remains the go-to repository for the documentary remains of Vilnius Jewry; it was certainly recognised as such by Sutzkever, Kaczerginski, and others who risked so much for these documents. It's a moral reality that influences the historical account: the documents in Lithuania are almost always referred to as "YIVO material" without qualification, including in many scholarly accounts. (Even Lithuanian officials, when agreeing to send the material to New York in the 1990s, seem to have been under the impression that all or at least most of it was YIVO's.) It's admirable, this marker of survival, but also poignant, as it puts into relief all that was lost. It flattens the sprawling, vibrant story of the origins of these documents, which is the sprawling, vibrant story of a city, a culture, a people. That YIVO survived is inspiring; that it's the only institution to have survived is heartrending.

That YIVO survived is inspiring; that it's the the only institution to have survived is heartrending

Lithuania's counterclaim is, simply, that all of the material – even what had indisputably been YIVO's – is part of Lithuanian heritage, and therefore belongs to and in Lithuania. (Zingeris and other officials have sometimes argued – though who knows how seriously – that the material in New York is rightfully theirs too.)

A parallel argument is that the contemporary Jewish community in Lithuania is the spiritual heir to the pre-war Jewish community, and that this material is part of its legacy.

This position might have some legal merit – none of this has ever been adjudicated, in Lithuania or in the United States, and restitution laws are notoriously thorny and internationally inconsistent – but is somewhat undermined by the fact that, for decades, these documents were not properly cared for, were not properly stored, preserved or processed. They were not treated, in other words, as Lithuanian heritage. This wasn't due to any overt antisemitic policy; it was simply overlooked for so long, negligence that can at least in part be explained by a lack of resources and, especially, a lack of qualified librarians and researchers. The Jewish community of Lithuania is tiny, maybe 5000 or 6000 people, and there just isn't much happening in terms of Jewish culture or scholarship. Community isn't defined solely by location: there were Jews in Vilnius before the war and Jews in Vilnius after the war, but that doesn't mean there's continuity. There are even questions of basic geography at play – before World War II, Vilnius, of course, was part of Poland. And in fact, after YIVO took possession of the crates from Offenbach, the Central Committee of Polish Jews initiated action to force their return – not to Vilnius, by then part of Lithuania, but to Poland. When the Allies distributed what had been designated as "heirless Jewish property", one of the chief considerations was utility – where would the books be read, the documents studied, the artefacts used. And YIVO was an explicitly transnational institution, as Yiddish is a transnational language. That it had been headquartered in Vilnius had less to do with the city per se than the people, the culture, the vibrancy that existed there – and are no longer there.

The foundational principles of modern archival science – which emphasise the preservation of an archive's context and order – are hardly clarifying in this instance. The material was heaped indiscriminately in Frankfurt; heaped again in the ghetto; then again in the Jewish Museum; then again in the Book Chamber. The old archives were in a sense destroyed – that is to say, the archives themselves, as an organisational unit, rather than their contents – and new ones were constituted.

Practically speaking, it's all moot anyway. It doesn't matter how legally or morally persuasive YIVO's claim is, because Lithuania is a sovereign state, and can more or less do what it wants. In certain cases, with certain countries, diplomatic pressure can be effective: Israel, for example, successfully lobbied the city of Worms to surrender the Worms Mahzor, a priceless illuminated codex from the thirteenth century. YIVO, however, has little political clout. And a lawsuit would be lengthy, expensive and unlikely to amount to anything beyond, at best, a moral victory. First a US court would have to agree that it has jurisdiction, and even if YIVO won the ensuing trial – hardly guaranteed – there are no real means to force compliance. (The State Department is generally very reluctant to jeopardise diplomatic relations on behalf of private individuals and institutions.) In 2004, Chabad successfully sued Russia in the US Federal Court for the return of its archive, but Russia simply refused to recognise the court's authority, prompting a judge in 2013 to issue contempt sanctions of $50,000 a day; Russia ignored this, too.

I asked Michael Kurtz, author of *America and the Return of Nazi Contraband*, what he thought YIVO's chances were of ever retrieving the material. "Zero," he said. "In this case, possession is ten-tenths of the law."

*

Only in 2012 was there a rapprochement. Brent, YIVO's current executive director, had gone to Vilnius, seen the sorry state the documents were in and understood what was in danger of being irretrievably lost. Moved, he met with Zingeris, who was still a member of parliament and the most politically powerful Jew in the country. Zingeris's stance hadn't changed – this was Lithuanian heritage, it belonged in Lithuania, YIVO should relocate, and so on. But Brent didn't demand Lithuania give up the material. Instead, he proposed they set aside the question of ownership – "We were fighting over the documents like the two prostitutes fighting in the story of Solomon," he told me – and work together to preserve, scan and share the material digitally. (In his previous job at Yale University Press, Brent had helped spearhead the digitisation of Stalin's personal archive.) Zingeris, enthusiastic, made the requisite connections.

An agreement was hammered out between YIVO and the Central State Archives; later, parallel agreements were made with the National Library of Lithuania and the Wroblewski Library of the Lithuanian Academy of Sciences. It was, in a sense, an updated and expanded digital version of the agreement made in the 1990s: the archives and documents – more than 400,000 in Vilnius and more than a million in New York, plus more than 12,000 books – would be digitised and uploaded to a central site. The project would take an estimated seven years to complete and cost more than US$5 million. Nearly all of it would be funded by YIVO.

The agreement, when it was announced, had its share of critics. Some felt that it was unconscionable to work, in any capacity, with the Lithuanian government, which has a spotty record when it comes to issues of Jewish history, particularly regarding Lithuanian complicity in the Holocaust. It was, in part, an issue of optics: YIVO would now be giving Lithuania an imprimatur of responsible behaviour with respect to Jews and Jewish history – a PR coup – while asking basically nothing in return. In effect, all Lithuania had to do was allow YIVO to pay for the digitisation of documents that were (at least in part) YIVO's. It was as if, critics said, Lithuania had been holding these documents hostage, and now the ransom was being paid. "It was a complete appeasement," said a former YIVO board member who asked not to be identified.

Nonetheless, the project launched in 2015. Dedicated teams in Vilnius and New York worked independently – though YIVO librarians travelled frequently to Vilnius – to preserve, process and digitise the material. The Lithuanians sent the images to New York (on hard drives, in the early stages, hand-carried by YIVO staff) – where they were quality-checked and uploaded, then given descriptions and keywords, providing the connective tissue between the collections. In 2016, Lithuania's National

"This is the most significant event in Jewish scholarship since the discovery of the Dead Sea Scrolls"

Library completed a renovation, and while moving books from the Book Chamber to the library, more documents turned up. These became part of the National Library's Judaica collection, under the auspices of the newly formed Judaica Research Centre, headed by Lara Lempert. Jonathan Brent and Suzanne Leon, then YIVO's director of development, raised nearly the entire budget for the digitisation effort, anchored by a multi-million-dollar gift from Edward Blank, a telemarketing pioneer. In 2017, another trove of documents was discovered in the manuscript collection at the National Library, and the project was extended so these could be digitised too.

*

By the time the Edward Blank YIVO Vilna Online Collections project is completed, in early 2022, more than one and a half million pages, from four institutions in two countries, will have been preserved and uploaded. "This material is stunningly important, and there is a great deal of it," Jack Jacobs, the professor and former Fulbright scholar, said. "It will radically impact any number of disciplines, from history to literature to folklore." A growing list of remarkable documents has been excavated – a notebook containing drafts of poems Sutzkever wrote in the ghetto, for example, and the diary of Beba Epstein, a fifth-grader living in Vilnius in the 1930s – and collectively the material will reshape our understanding of Jewish life in Eastern Europe before the war. Glenn Dynner, a historian and professor at New York's Sarah Lawrence College, described to me how recently unearthed documents upend prevailing narratives of pogroms, for instance – eyewitness accounts from the Ukrainian pogroms of 1919 attest to female pogrom leaders and Jewish self-defence initiatives. There are documents that have never been seen, and there are documents that only now, in context, make sense: more than one researcher I spoke to used the metaphor of puzzle pieces being put together. Lara Lempert told me that there are documents whose pages were scattered in four different locations, and have now been assembled online.

"Simply put," said David Fishman, author of *The Book Smugglers: Partisans, Poets and the Race to Save Jewish Treasures from the Nazis*, "this is the most significant event in Jewish scholarship since the discovery of the Dead Sea Scrolls."

The question of ownership remains undecided, though by design, suspended Talmudically in a state of non-resolution. (A celebrated online exhibition of Beba Epstein's memoir credits the

Lithuanian National Library as the "custodian" of the document.) But the agreement, even if not technically a concession on YIVO's part, functionally ratifies Lithuania's claim: they have gotten away without recognising this material as YIVO's, let alone returning it. (YIVO would not allow me to read the agreement, claiming that it is part of their institutional archives and thus not available to the public for fifty years. When I asked Lithuanian librarians about the dispute, they said they were unaware that YIVO had even made a claim on the material. Brent, when I told him this, expressed satisfaction, saying that it demonstrated just how effectively the question of ownership had been "bracketed".) "As a scholar I'm overjoyed," Fishman said, "but as a Jew, I'm heartbroken." And some of that early criticism has arguably been borne out: Lithuania has touted the project to a degree that feels borderline propagandistic – pushing out a steady stream of PR releases, awarding Brent the Cross of the Knight of the Order for Merits to Lithuania – but most of the scholars I spoke to agreed that, overall, Lithuania's commitment to the project, even if self-serving, constitutes progress.

The story of these objects is a material story: these books, these documents, were smuggled, hidden, buried, unburied, salavaged

It's not a resolution, then, but is, pragmatically, the best-case scenario for these miraculously surviving remnants of Eastern European Jewry. Lithuania was never going to give up the material, but now the originals are preserved, with high-resolution scans available online. "If I can obtain access, read, make use of – that suffices," said Jacobs, who sits on the board of the Claims

Conference – an organisation that negotiates with governments on behalf of Holocaust survivors – and is only too familiar with the hopelessness of most restitution claims. "I'm not a fetishist."

There are downsides to digitisation – any iteration introduces errors, and important paratextual information, like a handwritten note on the back of the document, may not be captured – but most researchers consider these trade-offs acceptable. Though there is also something discomfiting about holding up digital scans as satisfactory, or even superior, substitutes for the original. Maybe, in terms of scholarship, all that matters is being able to read the document – who cares if it's on a screen? But scholarship is hardly the only metric. The story of these objects is a material story: these books, these documents, were smuggled, hidden, buried, unburied, salvaged. Their story is imprinted onto them, and it's a story that can be experienced, or felt, or intuited, only in nonvirtual proximity. They are not unlike art, in that sense, or any objects with extratextual historical or sentimental value.

Cecile Kuznitz, professor of history at New York's Bard College and author of *YIVO and the Making of Modern Jewish Culture*, told me a revealing anecdote about going through YIVO microfilm and seeing scans of multiple copies of the same booklet. The duplicates had been included because, she learned, one of the copies contained a handwritten note from Sutzkever saying that it had been hidden in the Vilna ghetto. Nothing changed in terms of that booklet's content, but it has a legacy that isn't scannable. "Every surviving book from that world," wrote American historian Lucy Dawidowicz about what she saw in the depot in Offenbach, "had become a historical document, a cultural artifact, specimen, and testament of a murdered civilization."

While reporting this story, I visited the National Library in Vilnius, and Lempert showed me Beba Epstein's memoir. And in New York, the YIVO archivist brought out a handwritten diary of Theodore Herzl; the record book from the Vilna Gaon's synagogue; fragments from the earliest manuscript of *The Dybbuk*; and pages of Herman Kruk's diary, written in the Vilna ghetto. The power of these documents was immense – especially, for me, Kruk's diary. I had spent years researching the Vilna Ghetto, and had gone through the published version of the diary countless times. I was intimately familiar with the content, from his careful, loving descriptions of the ghetto library to his interactions with Jacob Gens, the ghetto chief. But I was wholly unprepared for the sensation of seeing it, touching it.

And then the archivist put it back in the stacks, where it will remain, because it is fragile, and because it is now on the internet. ≡

Love and restitution

The vanished world of my family's hotel

Rachel Kadish

The long scrape of a skate on a frozen pond. Lamplight, cast onto the snow through lace-curtained windows.

Horses' hooves, thudding.

In the sled, under robes, ride the elder Herzigs. Behind, tethered to the sled by tow-ropes, ski the Herzig daughters – perhaps all four, perhaps only two or three. The sisters shout to each other, eyes watering from cold wind and laughter as they weave between the horses' droppings.

In the summer there is tennis. Hiking. Five-thirty dancing. Chopin and Dvořák and news broadcasts, all emanating from the cabinet-sized radio, polished as a piano.

Let me try again.

Sled, horses, dancing.

If ink on paper can reassemble a world. If the shards of detail, gathered with care, can constitute a vessel to hold her heartbreak, and her heart.

Hotel Kryniczanka: French doors, lace curtains, tiers of balconies edged by delicate metalwork. Elegant table settings, pressed linens. A kosher kitchen. The Herzigs – the owners of the hotel – keep the room above the entryway for their frequent visits from Kraków. The other seventy rooms accommodate the guests drawn to this spa town in the Beskid Mountains, just a short drive from the Polish–Czechoslovakian border.

The Herzigs are orthodox but, where possible, turn a blind eye to their daughters' occasional rule-breaking. They've allowed their third daughter, an exceptional student, to graduate from high school at sixteen, a feat requiring a special ruling in a Kraków court. Rose: a blue-eyed, fair-haired beauty, a gymnast, a dancer. A quick-burning fuse of a spirit. She organises a co-ed hike on which young men and women, clad in bathing suits, smile for photographs from the middle of a stream. She arranges a trip to Yugoslavia; her mother and one sister trail her as uninvited chaperones – the Herzigs' tolerance has limits. After her early graduation, she studies law at Kraków's famed Jagiellonian University – a thing unheard of for a young woman.

The wedding of the eldest Herzig sister takes place in Hotel Kryniczanka's ballroom. Months of assembling trousseaus, then festivities spanning days, ending with the youngest sister asleep on two chairs pushed together on the side of the dance floor as the orchestra plays on.

Somewhere in that time Rose determines that, unlike her eldest sister with her arranged marriage, she'll choose her own husband.

What I know about the lives they lived at Hotel Kryniczanka and in Kraków I know not from my grandmother, Rose, but from the girl who slept on those pushed-together chairs – Rose's younger sister, my great-aunt Lilly. It was Lilly who told me about Rose's heartbreak when her first love – Felek, the soulful, quick-witted high school classmate everyone assumed she would marry – left her. And about Rose's engagement, and her wedding in June of 1938, to a brilliant, stubborn man eleven years her senior – my grandfather, Emek.

1939. The news of the mobilisation of the Polish army reaches Hotel Kryniczanka just after five-thirty dancing. Hitler's invasion is now inevitable. The Herzig family gathers to discuss plans.

My great-aunt's stories and a memoir left by my grandfather describe the following weeks and months and then years on the run. The bomb-cratered roads. Nights spent sleeping in barns, in coffins at an undertaker's. Their capture while attempting to cross the Lithuanian–Russian border. The Russian prison camp, the family's improbable escape. Then Kovno and the acquisition of illegal visas from Japanese diplomat Chiune Sugihara, who defied his government's orders in order to save refugees' lives. The escape via the Trans-Siberian Express to Japan; the Pacific crossing. And – after the ship, in accordance with F.D.R.'s policies, was denied permission to disgorge its refugees at every stop along the California coast – on to Mexico, where my family lived illegally for two years. Then finally, after the birth of my mother in Mexico City, on to the United States and to New York City.

Ten of them escape together, ranging in age from Rose's parents to her one-year-old niece; they rejoin four family members

Hotel Kryniczanka, c. 1929–1939

who emerged by other routes. The survival of fourteen from one family is exceedingly rare.

Back in Poland, 90 per cent of Poland's Jews – 90 per cent of the guests of Hotel Kryniczanka – were murdered. Out of my grandmother's Jewish high school class, only a small minority survived the war. In Kraków, Rose's cousin Itzik Stern worked desperately to orchestrate the protection of Jews through Oskar Schindler's factories. Still, family members died in Kraków's Podgórze ghetto. Family members died in Auschwitz. Rose's grandmother was shot in the back when she didn't descend a staircase fast enough. Rose's cousin Henia hid with her two young daughters in the countryside. When Henia ran out of money to pay the Polish farmer who was hiding them, he threatened to hack her and her daughters to pieces with his axe. She tried desperately to find money. She failed. The farmer followed through on his threat.

For decades after the war, thirteen of the fourteen relatives who had survived lived within a few Manhattan blocks of one another. While my father was posted overseas with the Air Force, my mother, my sister and I (our brother wasn't yet born) lived with our grandparents. Later, after my father was home, we'd visit my grandparents almost every week.

By then my grandmother was only in her fifties, and had been ill for twenty years. Too sick to shop for her grandchildren on short notice, she kept a closet stocked with gifts. Her pulmonary disease, in those days treated with strong doses of steroids, left her red-eyed and moon-faced. She had a "sick room" where she slept so her coughing wouldn't keep my grandfather awake at night, and in this narrow room with its single bed she wrote poetry in Hebrew – the language she hoped to use in the near future, when they would finally leave Manhattan to move into the apartment they had bought in Jerusalem.

In fact she would never be well enough to make the move – not even when both her older sisters did, or when one of her daughters did.

The prodigious effort she put into rallying for our visits was invisible to me. Years later, I'd recall this with shame. On entering the apartment with my older sister, I'd run directly to the closet, forgetting my mother's cautionary whisper: *Grandma's been sick and might not have had time.* Somehow my grandmother was always prepared – she would swing the closet door open to reveal some new treasure: a doll, or a book of fairytales, or crepe paper and pipe cleaners to make the flowers with which she helped us festoon our under-the-dining-room-table cave.

It was through her mispronunciations that I realised, at age four, that there were two different ways to pronounce "the" – and that I somehow knew how to navigate the mysteries of "thuh" and "thee", whereas my grandmother quietly read to me from "Thee Princess and thee Pea" and "Thee Little Match Girl". I knew that I did not want the superiority this wisdom conferred on me. Just as I did not wish to bear witness – sitting in the crook of her arm, my head against her side so that I nodded gently, involuntarily, with her threadbare breaths – while thee little match girl died alone, just out of reach of the warmth that could have saved her.

What did I know of her? That she loved me. That I wanted her not to suffer.

Together we leave the bright marzipan wonderland of an Upper West Side bakery, my fingers twined in the red-and-white-striped string of the cardboard parcel with which I've been entrusted. My grandmother glances at the clouds: rain. Carefully she withdraws two plastic rain bonnets from her handbag. She puts on her own, then with a gentle motion cocoons my head and secures the tie beneath my chin. A bow, knotted tight. The loud slide of my own hair against the plastic. The sounds echo inside the rain bonnet, thunder in my ears.

As a child I knew nothing of my relatives' attempts to reclaim Hotel Kryniczanka and various family members' homes in Kraków. Even when I became aware of the effort as a young adult, I asked little about it, preferring to focus on their accounts of life before and during the war. While I often disagreed with my grandfather's politics, and – to his delight – sometimes sparred with him, I felt more strongly with each passing year the urgency of his refrain: *you need to remember these stories, because someday we'll be gone.*

The family's restitution claim, if mentioned, was a topic that elicited weary sighs. Some sort of token restitution payment, my great-aunt Lilly said, had been issued by Poland after the war; apparently this made it less likely that any subsequent claim approaching the property's real value would succeed. But my relatives held out hope that they might be able to reclaim Hotel Kryniczanka.

Since 1948, the town of Krynica-Zdrój had been using the hotel building as the town's high school. Over the years, my relatives made attempts to re-establish ownership – yet the case languished. They couldn't know for certain how much of the delay was due to the slowness of the Polish court system, or the complexities that followed the nationalisation of property under Communism. To them, the delays seemed a deliberate tactic on the part of Poles using the properties of Holocaust survivors: if cases dragged on long enough, the survivors would die, and their heirs would lack the interest or language skills to persist.

For my relatives, the heart of the issue wasn't money. Unlike so many seeking restitution for history's atrocities, they were fortunate to have had education and connections that helped them build new lives. But their world had been annihilated. Amid a sea of irreparable losses, something as concrete as the theft of a building could still be remedied. What would be regained was more than a deed. It was, for my relatives, home. And there was something else: in the opening months of the occupation, the Nazis' General Government in Poland had officially claimed Hotel Kryniczanka as an "ownerless" property. The beds once slept in by Hotel Kryniczanka's murdered Jewish guests had been used by Nazi soldiers. Regaining ownership would reverse a desecration.

The first time I met Felek was at a small Holocaust Studies conference in Manhattan in the early 1990s. He'd come from London to deliver the keynote address, and my mother and great-aunt Lilly wanted me to meet him. I took the subway between graduate school classes.

The speakers so far that afternoon had addressed the audience in professorial drones. Now here was Felek at the podium: slight, soft-spoken, riveting. Nearly eighty years old, he could have been a diminutive Polish Walter Matthau, his eyes alert, his face expressively weathered. Unlike the other presenters, Felek wasn't an academic. He was an art dealer and printer who had made it his personal mission to document and memorialise Poland's Jewish community. As he read letters and poems written by the doomed Jews of the Kraków ghetto – artefacts he'd helped salvage and organise after the war – his grief was audible, his voice at times barely above a murmur, and the room woke palpably, painfully, to the words of the lost.

When he finished speaking, the room seemed suffused with his tender intonations. People touched his shoulder as he made his way down the aisle. They detained him, wanting a word. Finally he reached Lilly and my mother, who introduced me. His eyes still shining, he greeted me with a brimming silence. "I could have been your grandfather," he said at last. "But your grandmother chose much better."

Then he told me: "I credit your grandmother with saving my life."

That was the first of three times Felek told me his and Rose's love story. The version he offered that afternoon in New York was brief – we had only a few minutes before responsibilities took him elsewhere. But he imparted the facts with startling gravity. He and Rose had dated for two years in Kraków. In those days you did not date for two years without intent to marry. But he was young, he wasn't ready. So he ran off. He went to study in London, a choice many of his friends found bewildering – why would any Krakovian go elsewhere when the renowned Jagiellonian University was right there in Kraków?

When, at dawn on 1 September 1939, Hitler's planes roared into Polish airspace, Felek was safely in London.

Those of us who grew up with survivors know what it is to step gingerly around their pain. Many of us feel haunted by their stories, still more by their silences. Their eloquent hand gestures subsiding into reverie; and always, their caution.

Those who'd known Rose best often found it difficult to speak of her. They'd say a few words about the feisty young woman she'd been, and then … a grimace of pain. She had died at the age of fifty-nine. Where her story should have been, there was a void.

I was five years old when my grandmother died. Shortly after, I began having a recurring nightmare, which continued through my twenties. In the dream, I go back to the apartment building in New York City where my grandparents lived. But the building is deserted. I'm too late. They've all been taken. I climb the dark stairs, rounding every landing, searching. My steps echo. Nothing, nothing. Nothing. Only an empty dress – my grandmother's – dangling on a hanger in the stairwell.

I wake wanting the impossible: to go back into the nightmare and find her.

My grandfather was a charming disputant and a commanding story-teller. Born in 1905 into a Kraków family of modest means, Emek worked his way through a PhD in philosophy at the Jagiellonian University, then changed course in the early 1930s to study medicine. His studies were punctuated by turmoil. Antisemitic student groups attempted to force Jews out of student organisations and make them stand or sit at the backs of lecture halls. The medical school forbade Jewish students to perform dissections on non-Jewish corpses; if Jewish students failed to supply Jewish corpses to the prosectorium, they would fail out of medical school. My grandfather led the student protests, publicised what was happening through the Jewish newspaper, and eventually succeeded in reversing the medical school's policy.

His leadership also took directions then considered quixotic. In 1934, persuaded that the hoped-for Jewish state would need a navy, shipping capacity and commercial fishermen, he founded an organisation called Zebulun to train Jews in seamanship, with chapters in Kraków, the port city Gdynia and elsewhere.

Emek met Rose when she clerked at his brother's Kraków law office. At first, the attention of a man in his thirties embarrassed her. Undeterred, he took himself to Hotel Kryniczanka for a weekend. When he injured his knee skiing and was confined to bed for two weeks, Rose took care of him.

And that, my grandfather wrote in his memoirs, *was that.*

They were married in the hotel's ballroom.

In his old age in Jerusalem, after he'd shut his medical practice and left New York City, Emek typed his memoirs onto pale blue aerogrammes, which he sent to my mother each week. Fiercely intellectual, my grandfather spoke an erudite English. During the war, he'd made good use of his facility with languages, becoming fluent enough to deliver speeches in Spanish during their two years in Mexico and swiftly mastering English on his arrival in the United States. Later, in Jerusalem, his routine included Saturday-evening Torah study in Hebrew with a small group that included Menachem Begin. He often admonished his American grandchildren for our ignorance of Greek and Latin.

In my grandfather's aerogrammes, the story of the family's flight appears in long, declarative paragraphs punctuated by occasional philosophical musings – the hallmark of the man I remember: stubborn, wryly humorous, disinclined to traffic in delicate feelings. He is clear about his Polish patriotism – when Hitler invaded, he volunteered as a physician for the Polish army and narrowly escaped being shot alongside thousands of fellow officers in the Katyn massacre, a mass killing Stalin authorised to wipe out not only Poland's military leadership but also its educated class. He is clear, too, about his sense of betrayal when, on the roads fleeing German attack, his Catholic colleagues made plain that they didn't want a Jew joining them on their wagon.

Ever-present in his memoirs is a bland paternalism common in European gentlemen of his generation. After the chapter about their courtship, Rose mainly disappears into the shadows of his accounts. Rarely does she receive more than a passing mention in his description of their wartime travails, though now and then he notes that, with her fair hair and Slavic looks, Rose would go out alone to scout for food or supplies while other, more Jewish-looking family members stayed hidden.

There is one moment, though, when his narrative lingers on Rose. Sometimes it seems to me that he left the words there for us, a stand-in for other things he could not name.

He writes here of their weeks in a Russian prison, after their group of ten family members was captured crossing the Lithuanian border:

[We] were called for the usual interrogation which included repeated thorough body inspection and rectal and vaginal exam-inations … We went into the big house where Mother and Rose were again interrogated. I was left alone in the big hall … After a few hours they escorted us back to our prison … Rose suddenly found herself in a world of nightmares. She was sitting there on the cot with wide open eyes, looking into space and repeating in a moaning voice: "They are going to execute my father, he is being executed, my God, they are executing him." This was going on for hours and no amount of reassurance by her parents and myself could break the nightmare. I was desperate and felt com-pletely defeated. After hours of fruitless effort to bring Rose back to her "senses" I went to the corner of the room and cried. Finally Rose fell on the cot and was asleep. After several hours of deep sleep Rose woke up fresh and relaxed, cheerful and optimistic, again her youthful self. The crisis was over.

It is the only moment in the memoir – a tale of four continents, the losses of his larger family, his culture and his world – when he cries. My grandfather: a man who would not come to the breakfast table until he'd dressed in suit and tie. Who, for all his linguistic skill, would never develop the ability to speak about emotion or vulnerability – his own or other people's.

Not until my mid-twenties, when a friend recommended Helen Epstein's *Children of the Holocaust: Conversations with Sons and Daughters of Survivors,* did I encounter stories that matched my mother's and aunt's accounts of Rose's moments of despair during their childhood in New York City.

It was a strange and terrible comfort, learning that my grandmother wasn't alone, that there were other mothers and grandmothers who had miraculously survived the war, but had not emerged whole. Epstein's interviewees repeated things I'd heard about my grandmother almost verbatim. "She barricaded herself in the bathroom for hours … My mother was crying. 'I don't want to go on anymore. I can't stand it.'"

Rose, locking herself in the bathroom, weeping. Opening windows to look down from vertiginous heights that could at last free her. She can no longer stand it, no longer go on. But each time, she does. She unlocks the bathroom door and emerges to cook, to do what's needed.

My grandfather, unable to fix her suffering or endure it, absents himself.

Hotel Kryniczanka: light through French doors, through the intricate metalwork railings. On one side, the balconies overlook the broad street, covered now in a dusting of snow. On the other flows the Kryniczanka stream, ice crusting its edges. From a footbridge above the wooded stream, the hotel's dance orchestra is faintly audible. Through mullioned panes, through lace-curtained windows, the dancers flash by in their festive dress – whirling, circling. The warmth of the gathering just out of reach.

Beginning in my twenties, I read all I could about Poland. I wanted to understand my relatives' love for Poland, because it seemed to me that it was love – despite all – that shone through my grandfather's references to Polish poetry and history. I also began gravitating towards bridge-builders, participating in German–Jewish dialogues, listening hard whenever someone seemed to be attempting repair.

In those days – the mid-1990s – reparation and restitution were much in the news, often described in anodyne language referring to *justice*. It seemed to me, though, that whatever was being served up in a reparation claim, it wasn't justice – justice being impossible in any meaningful sense. The subject cried out for a different sort of conversation. What, if anything, did a reparation claim repair? What did restitution promise – and did it deliver on that promise?

But during those years I didn't question my older relatives about the restitution claim; that seemed like their private business, their private pain.

The second time Felek told me his and Rose's love story was in Kraków, in 1998.

I'd travelled to Poland with my mother to join a handful of our relatives from Jerusalem at the Kraków Jewish Cultural Festival. Every summer during the festival, the neighborhood that was once the city's hub of Jewish life would come alive with klezmer and cantorial music and presentations on Jewish topics. The festival attracted thousands of visitors – among them Felek, who travelled from his home in London. As one of the few Kraków survivors to return, Felek played a central role, guiding students and tourists through a Jewish world few alive could still navigate.

The first afternoon, Felek walked my family into Jama Michalika, a centuries-old café off Kraków's main square. Behind thick doors, the rooms were lined with artwork, the carved furnishings ornate and heavily elegant. Felek ushered us towards the back of the café. Stepping aside at one narrow passage, he gestured my mother and aunts ahead. As I passed, he set a hand on my arm, slowing me. "You know," he said, "your grandmother was a remarkable woman."

He chose a spot for us to settle: a round wooden table surrounded by chairs and a green velvet sofa. "This," he said, "is the table." He turned to my elderly relative Regina, who had been my grandmother's best friend in high school. (Like Felek, Regina and her husband were out of the country when Hitler invaded.) To Regina he said, "She sat where you're sitting."

We ordered kremówka, a sweet, Napoleon-like pastry that slipped under the fork.

"She cried," Felek said.

I was the youngest family member present – twenty-eight, not much older than Felek and Rose when they'd sat at this spot. Felek laid a dark-veined hand over mine and addressed his story to me. "I was young, and not ready to marry. I was frightened. I thought your grandmother's family – it was a wealthy family, you know – would swallow me up." He hesitated before continuing. "I wasn't good to her."

His eyes were shining. We'd all set down our forks and coffee cups.

"She cried so hard. I didn't know what to do." He turned to Regina. "I went to get you, but you weren't home. And it's good you weren't home, it's good –" he shook his head "– because I shouldn't have involved you."

Slowly he tapped the table with the tips of his fingers, each touch a caress. "When I came back to this spot, she was gone."

My great-aunt Lilly, who had known Felek since girlhood, said to me once that when Felek jilted my grandmother, it broke both their hearts. *Both*, my great-aunt said. *Not only your grandmother's. Everyone could see it. Everyone thought they should marry.* Felek had remained in Poland through Rose's long courtship with my grandfather. The spring when Rose and Emek finally married, Felek moved to England.

"This is life," he said softly. "A mad dance of atoms."

When Felek had finished his story, there was a long silence. He turned to me and softly repeated a line that I could by then have recited alongside him. "Your grandmother was a remarkable woman. I've not met her equal. I credit her with saving my life."

We met several times that week. At meals Felek sang softly in Polish with my relatives. Strolling past elegant, soot-darkened apartment buildings, he would direct my attention to curtained windows on upper floors – the bedrooms of friends killed in the war. He spoke of being a foreign correspondent in London for the Polish Jewish paper *Nowy Dziennik*. Just weeks before Hitler's invasion of Poland, in early August of 1939, Felek wrote for the paper, "I stake my journalistic reputation on the prediction that there will be no war."

Working with the Polish government in exile in wartime London, Felek was present when the first report of the death camps came through in a message from the Polish underground. When Felek spoke to me about that day, he told me he'd refused those devastating words instinctively; he took the telegram and wrote atop it, "This is not true."

In an essay Felek wrote about those events, however, he reported only the reaction of the other Jew in the room – Ignacy Schwarzbart, then the sole Jewish member of the Polish National Council in London: "[Schwarzbart] wrote, with a trembling hand, in his diary: 'This is not possible.'"

I can't explain the difference between these accounts, though I've since confirmed that Felek told at least one other person the same story he told me. What seems clear is that whoever penned the rejection of that cataclysmic news, Felek felt deeply responsible.

"There has not been a day in my life that I have not reverted in my thoughts to those events," Felek wrote. "The generation of Jews of the post-Holocaust era, the 'survivors' in the broadest sense, are a people apart. Burdened by their memory, walking-wounded, in eternal mourning. I do not think that an outsider can understand this condition."

Of Felek's large extended family, only he and his mother would survive the war.

He has Weltschmerz, my great-aunt Lilly would later say of him. World-sorrow.

On a narrow street we stood speaking long after a late lunch. Felek, who had once been a follower of Jabotinsky, told me that his decision not to move to Israel after the war had burned bridges with some of the surviving members of his community. When Felek visited Israel, Menachem Begin – his friend from pre-war Zionist circles – had called him a tourist and refused to shake his hand.

Felek had had his reasons for not moving to Israel, yes. "But Begin was right," he said. "I did not contribute." He stood another moment. "This is life," he said softly. "A mad dance of atoms." Slowly he buttoned his sweater.

Rose Herzig, c. 1936

That week in Kraków Felek was seemingly everywhere, offering himself up tirelessly to those who flocked to the festival. The words "Felek sent me" were enough to swing wide the doors to a sold-out concert; to prompt busy people to clear time in their schedules for meetings. He told his stories on the cobbled streets; in the square; along the river. A gracious ancient mariner, cursed to return every summer to recite his story – eternal penance for his escape. Nothing would bring Kraków's Jewish community back, but with each recitation he rebuilt it in words, a small act of restitution.

"I remain an unregenerate agnostic, thank God," wrote Felek in his book of essays, *Poland, What Have I to Do with Thee*. "This serves me reasonably well by day, if not so well by night." In place of a conventional religious faith, he seemed to have set an eternal flame of a different sort. If at that first wartime confrontation with the truth he'd been disbelieving, he'd devoted himself thereafter to documenting the calamity that had befallen his community. After World War II, Felek had worked on the interrogation of war criminals with British military intelligence. He'd gone on to write and present to audiences in England, Poland, Israel and the United States about the fates of Poland's Jews, while simultaneously acknowledging the suffering of his non-Jewish compatriots. He referred to Poles and Jews as "the two saddest nations on earth" and expressed his admiration for Polish courage.

Repeatedly, Felek stepped into terrain too fraught for others to tread. He did not excuse Artek – a high school classmate who had done the Germans' bidding as a member of the Jewish Police, and who was later killed by Jews for his collaboration – but cautioned that "one must remember that before he was sent out on his deadly hunt to fill the quota of victims, he was told in no uncertain terms that should he return empty-handed, his father or mother, his sister or his brother would be killed instead. Let those who can pass a moral judgement." For years, the survivor community had spoken of a Nazi soldier who'd once carried a Leica illegally into the Warsaw Ghetto, snapping four rolls of film before his camera, with a fifth roll still in it, was confiscated. Felek tracked down the man and, without recrimination, persuaded him to hand over photographs that had lain unseen for decades – the only existing images of men, women and children soon to meet their deaths. Those searing images appear in *In the Warsaw Ghetto Summer 1941: Photographs by Willy Georg with Passages from Warsaw Ghetto Diaries*, with a wrenching afterword by Felek, in which he wrote,

> The people caught in these photographs – busy, feverish, emaciated, oppressed, but still living a life of sorts – are unaware of the unthinkably cruel end that awaits them shortly. Virtually none will escape a horrible death. One's instinct is to shout a word of warning – run! Hide! – but it is too late. At that stage nothing, but nothing, they could have done or left undone would have had the slightest effect on their fate.

No matter how many of Felek's speeches and essays I read, what I'd observed at that first speech in New York City remained true: he refused to package loss into a tidy, palatable form. His essays end in anguish, in endearment, in raw emotion.

"It is customary on occasions like this," he said at the Polish Cultural Centre in London, on the fiftieth anniversary of the Warsaw Ghetto uprising,

> for the speaker to end on an uplifting note, with an accent on hope and optimism, as if to say that despite it all – and so on …

You must forgive me – I cannot rise to that. I stand helpless, orphaned, with a sense of an enormous, irreparable wrong. There is not a day in my life but that I think of this. I cannot forget, must not forget, don't want to forget. The world should also be made to remember.

He rebuffed the impulse towards the kind of neat summary that lets us turn away from the quicksilver souls of the lost. He asked his audience to stand with him in the tide.

Yet he spoke little about his pre-war existence to his non-Jewish wife in London, or to his children and grandchildren. He did not wish, he told me, to burden them.

To judge by the veneration with which Felek's name was spoken in Kraków, legions of students and tourists had been captivated by this man who so humbly bore his weight of sorrow. And part of Felek's tour, I learned, involved taking students to a certain centuries-old wood-panelled café off the main square. Sitting them at a table in the rear, telling them about a woman he'd left there crying.

Tourists and students I'd never met had heard my grandmother's story.

I refused to be troubled by it. If there was something unnerving about Felek's use of my grandmother's story – something scripted in the way he summoned her apparition at that back table of Café Jama Michalika, had her cry unstoppable tears for strangers while he himself teared up over how he'd once hurt her – so what? What did it matter how often or on what schedule Felek repeated the story? It was a flare of tenderness in an otherwise dark landscape, a story to fill the void. My grandmother had a hard life; now here was a piece of her heartbreak recast in redemptive light, made meaningful – because however sad a role she'd played in this tale, it had helped save the life of this gentle man. Felek's regret over her pain was a salve that reached back and forward in time. Since childhood I'd wanted to find my grandmother. Here she was: loved, remembered.

Near the end of the festival week, my mother and I took the train south to Hotel Kryniczanka.

We'd been advised not to attempt entry. Usually I'm the cautious one, my mother stepping fearlessly ahead. This time I wanted to get closer, but she wouldn't budge.

We stood outside the building.

The hotel was as imposing as I'd imagined. Balconies; the old ballroom's mullioned panes; the windows of the Herzig family's former rooms above the entryway. Capacious old stables, now presumably used as garages. There was graffiti, yes; the walls were stained here and there. But the building's elegance was undeniable.

Students peered at us from classroom windows. I couldn't make out the faces of the teachers; surely some were old enough to remember when a pair of dark-haired women would not have seemed out of place on that street.

We lingered. But after taking photos, there was nothing more to do. We stood on the sidewalk for a while. Then left.

Years passed. Survivors grew older and frailer. Overdue tributes took place. The United States Holocaust Museum opened an exhibit about Chiune Sugihara's life-saving visas; one of my great-aunts contributed her visa for display. At a reception at the

Japanese embassy in Washington DC, my family was able to meet and thank Sugihara's widow and some of his family. Friends participated in a ceremony to honour the Poles who had saved them, despite the Nazi death penalty for Poles who aided Jews.

The work of repair could come in the most mundane exchanges, or the most fraught. In Jerusalem I watched two lanky German seminarians go to tragicomic lengths to avoid uttering a word of their native language in public, lest overhearing it cause pain among elderly strangers. In Kraków I met with a Polish priest who spoke with glimmering insight and sympathy for the position of the Jews in Poland. I spent hours in conversation with the non-Jewish head of the Kraków Jewish Cultural Centre and came away impressed by his devotion to a community that once numbered 56,000 and then stood at 120. I saw a Holocaust survivor reach out to a young German woman whose grandmother had been a member of the Nazi party.

I also saw flashes of exhaustion. Those who laboured hardest at the task of keeping the flame of memory alive sometimes seemed depleted – and small wonder. A human being is not a burning bush. We are consumed.

And inevitably there were moments when what looked like repair felt more like its opposite. In the old Jewish neighbourhood of Kraków – turned tourist destination after the release of Spielberg's *Schindler's List* – Judaica shops featured carved wooden figurines of Jews. I assumed the tourists who purchased them were unaware that the figurines were traditional Polish talismans: a wooden Jew was good luck for business. At an exhibit in the art gallery of the Jewish Cultural Centre, I was approached by a Polish sculptor so enamoured of Jewish faces – and presumably so unaware of the antisemitic stereotypes embodied in the trade in wooden Jew figurines – that she asked me to pose for her.

When I declined, she assured me that it didn't matter. Tapping her own temple, she told me that she'd already memorised my face.

The more I learned about restitution cases in Poland, the more complex the subject felt. It was true that victims' families had every right to their former homes. It was also true that many of the current Polish occupants had bought homes in good faith from those who had first taken the stolen property – and that some of those who'd originally moved into the homes of murdered Jews had themselves been displaced by war. Add to the mix the question of post-communist reprivatisation of properties, and the tangle seemed overwhelming. The specifics of restitution – the dollar figure put on loss, the desiccated legal language in the context of such annihilation – could feel like a defilement. And while the public conversation about claims featured sober and respectful voices, there were inevitably some who found in the issue an opportunity to self-aggrandise – to boast,

> *I found myself wishing that a plaque could simple be laid on every street corner where someone had been murdered:* This is what happened here

as did one lawyer, about making his German counterparts literally sweat, or about waiting outside a courthouse in the wind in a deliberately unzipped jacket – because in the concentration camps people *suffered*.

I found myself wishing that a plaque could simply be laid on every street corner where someone had been murdered: *This is what happened here.* A restitution, at least, of the truth. But I also hated the feeling that someone in Kraków or Krynica-Zdrój might be quietly hoping for the last of the Herzig sisters to die, so that they could proceed with a home repair or maybe add on a garage without fear of losing their investment.

What had been missing in all those news accounts about post-war claims confronted me now at every turn: restitution is hazardous terrain. The ground cries out for justice, but repair rarely looks like we expect. Success generally comes with an asterisk. We're buffeted by memory, anger, sometimes fantasy.

I wrote essays on the topic, yet struggled: the intricate legal and political landscape of restitution deserved analysis, but analytic language also missed the heart of the matter. Whether or not my family ever regained the deed to the hotel, there was a more personal kind of restitution I craved for them: a reversal of the erasure of their presence, their humanity, their stories.

And what I wanted to write for Rose, who, unlike the others, never had the chance to speak for herself, wasn't an analysis. It was a love letter – the sort that's the only gift we can offer to someone who has moved beyond our reach. *You are not forgotten.*

In 2001, three years after my visit with my mother, my brother and I walked through the doors of Hotel Kryniczanka – or rather, Krynica-Zdrój's high school: Liceum Ogólnokształcące im. Henryka Sucharskiego w Krynicy-Zdroju.

Whatever plan we'd discussed on the drive from Kraków, we discarded it on arrival. We simply slung our backpacks over our shoulders and entered.

There are moments when the senses become overloaded – when one's attention is so amplified that the too-bright world blurs and slides. We walked through the atrium, up the stairs. The light was liquid, sound magnified. Did we speak to each other? Syllables, maybe – *oh* – or *there* – or *look* – like undersea creatures moving through the depths, pinging softly to be sure of one another.

It took the students only seconds to become curious about us. Their alertness followed us through the building. It's possible that with his blue eyes and fairer colouring, my brother on his own might have passed for a Pole – but not standing next to me. And we were too old to be high school students, and then surely there were the thousand tiny things that give Americans away.

Long, narrow corridors, too-small classrooms – the size of hotel bedrooms. Every open door revealed a cross on the wall.

It meant too much. The seconds spun down too quickly. Another set of stairs, another floor. My brother and I tracked each other mutely: down corridors and back. Up more stairs. Students began to call out to us in broken English. Their teachers glanced at us and then away, as though interpreting the meaning of two strangers passing through their school wasn't in their job description.

It's a treacherous thing, tangling with restitution

It couldn't last – the students' curiosity was building. There would come a breaking point.

We descended the stairs and made one last turn, into a gymnasium plainly never designed to be a gymnasium. Large mullioned windows. Curtains shedding delicate lace patterns on the wooden floor – and everywhere, light. The ballroom in which our grandparents were married.

We didn't want to leave. We left.

The third time Felek told me the story was in London. I was glad that my travels would give me a chance to see him again, less than a year since we'd met in Kraków. Without the distractions of the festival and the large family group, I hoped to finally learn more about Rose as she'd once been – before the losses, before the war.

We sat in the café Felek had chosen – a brightly lit space, windows and white walls, small vases of flowers. There was an air of briskness about him that I at first attributed to his workday attire. We ordered tea. He asked after my family and I filled him in: news of the remaining Herzig sisters, of children and grandchildren scattered across three continents.

I suspect I was the first to mention my grandmother – confidently, with the feeling of performing a familiar ritual. But this time Felek's manner was reserved.

"Your grandmother loved me very much," he said, teacup in hand. Then, with a slight sigh, he concluded, "I myself, unfortunately, did not reciprocate."

A sharp bolt of betrayal. I muddled through the remainder of our conversation, dizzy from the reversal.

An hour later we left the café together, and I watched him recede into the rush-hour crowd: an indifferent angel vanishing amid the commuters. I could still feel the weight of the hand he laid on my shoulder before taking his leave – the same warm gesture as always, but this time I'd felt I was being warded off.

If he hadn't loved her, how to make sense of all of it? The repeated visits to the back table of the Kraków café, the evocation of my sobbing grandmother before rapt listeners – was that just survivor guilt, more *Weltschmerz*?

Jettisoning for a moment everything I knew about the complexity of the human heart, I strode through the crowd, propelled by my thoughts. He'd put my grandmother's heartbreak on display. If he was going to make my grandmother a monument to sorrow – so the furious arc of my logic went – he'd damn well better stand there right next to her and be a monument to sorrow, too. No dodging in and out of Kraków for the annual misty-eyed visit with her ghost … only to shake her off in London. Had it been in my power, I'd have acted the Biblical Jacob, called back the tweed-jacketed angel and barred his escape. *I will not let you go until you bless her.*

But already he was out of my reach, lost in the crowd.

If it were true that he hadn't loved her, then his choice to trot out her pain for tourists would have been cruel. And I didn't think he was cruel. Rather, he seemed to have drawn a protective cordon around himself.

A human being is not a burning bush.

To this day, I've met almost no one who has given as much to the task of Holocaust remembrance as Felek. In the process of rebuilding the world of Polish Jewry story by story, he'd even offered himself up as a monument – a statue frozen in a posture of grief.

It's a treacherous thing, tangling with restitution.

I couldn't reconcile Felek's earlier stories with the efficient way he'd shed my grandmother here in London – the tearful recitation with the tidy, distanced version. It seemed clear, however, that he'd now retreated; whatever might lie behind the ritual retelling or the romanticised *I credit her with saving my life,* the subject of my grandmother felt closed.

I choose to believe that he loved her. But however much I admired and appreciated Felek's work, he couldn't or wouldn't help me understand who Rose had been, when she'd been whole and healthy, when her world had not yet been destroyed.

I'd leave him in peace. Let him be haunted in his own way, and me in mine.

My grandmother by then had been gone more than twenty years. If the fragile spark of her life could be paid tribute in words, those words would have to be my own – a structure built not with timbers and stone, but with whatever fragmented stories I had at hand, and whatever tendrils of imagination might tie them together.

Only recently did I ask my mother if I could see the paperwork she had concerning the restitution claim on Hotel Kryniczanka. Her files cover just a portion of the case's long life – even so, they span decades. Inside are sheaves of correspondence, documents with raised seals, references to court proceedings, birth and death certificates. A list of lot sizes and number of rooms. The oldest documents bear the fine indentations of a typewriter; these give way to the orderly pointillism of a dot-matrix printer. Further along there are unreadable faded faxes, then printed emails. Paperclips have rusted, leaving long brown scoops on the top corners of documents. With time, the street the hotel is on is given a new name. The names of the hotel's owners – David and Mariem Herzig – are replaced by the names of their surviving daughters.

A document gives power of attorney to a Polish lawyer – and then in that same folder, a photocopy of a Polish newspaper article denounces the lawyer as a drunkard, a fraud without a legal degree, and an impersonator of Jews. (The article's breathlessly conspiratorial tone makes its accuracy seem questionable; all I know is that after his repeated requests for payment and repeated failure to produce results, my relatives lost trust in him.) There is correspondence with lawyers whose class-action lawsuit against Poland my family joined, or perhaps merely considered joining. Scattered newspaper clippings argue that Poland *can't* repay Jews for properties because of its economic duress – or, conversely, that Poland *must* repay in order to show clear property titles and reassure potential investors, thereby alleviating its economic duress. While my mother's files don't contain documentation of the earlier Polish restitution payment my relatives received (recently I was able to identify the source of that payment as the 1960 Polish Claims Program), there's discussion of what sounds like a 2001 attempt at legislation governing restitution, vetoed by the Polish president. And a restitution programme that seemed to offer resolution for Jewish survivors, but only provided they had been citizens of Poland on 31 December 1999.

> *Nested among dry legal documents, are letters between my relatives ... I linger here, amid their voices*

Further along, grouped across several folders, are letters addressed to two United States senators and one representative, an American ambassador to Poland, a Polish premier, an American under secretary of state, and two presidents – one American, one Polish. In each, my relatives politely describe the roadblocks they've encountered in pursuing claims on the homes they were forced to flee: multiple postponements by Polish courts, repeated requests for documents already submitted and accepted. They point out that the ranks of survivors are thinning, people dying without seeing any resolution. They describe what appears to be a deliberate slow-down of the process. They ask for help.

Folder after folder: the request for the return of one last tangible thing, in barren legal language that has no words for all that's irretrievable.

And here and there, nested among dry legal documents, are letters between my relatives – some connected to the case, some inserted into the files for no apparent reason. There is nothing from my grandmother. But I find my grandfather, and I find my great-aunts and even Felek: reaching out over the years, checking in about travel plans, sending warm greetings and occasional reflections on a piece of their shared past. I linger here, amid their voices.

The final manila folder in my mother's filing cabinet is thin. I delay opening it – after this there will be only silence.

The papers here are mostly from 2005. A burst of hopeful activity in that year concludes with advice from a consulting company in Poland: proceeding further is impossible without new laws regarding reprivatisation of assets stolen by the Nazis and later nationalised under Communism.

The final sheet of paper is a numb-sounding 2005 note from one family member to another: "... *at this time it would take a change of government ...*"

Felek died in 2003. His obituaries, appearing in *The Times*, *The Guardian*, *The Independent*, the Jewish Telegraphic Agency and elsewhere, described him variously as Jewish Kraków's "universally recognised chief remembrancer"; a "pioneer of Polish–Jewish reconciliation"; "kind, ethically scrupulous, much loved"; "the most lachrymose adult I have ever known"; and a man who "breathed contradictions".

The labours itemised in his obituaries seem limitless: books published with his support, organisations founded, collaborations midwived. (Only after accepting the assignment to write this essay did I discover that Felek helped found the Jewish Quarterly in London in 1953, and that for decades his essays regularly appeared in these pages.)

Following Felek's death, an award was given for several years by the Judaica Foundation in Kraków to recognise "outstanding achievement in preserving and making known the heritage of Polish Jewry". The award, presented in Kraków before an audience, was a figure cast in metal and wood: a statuette of Felek.

The Herzig sisters are gone now. Two of them lived to ninety-seven, one to ninety-nine. The last to die, in the winter of 2020, was the little girl who slept on pushed-together chairs at the edge of her sister's wedding celebration: my great-aunt Lilly.

With the passage of decades, the fourteen members of my family who made it out of Poland have grown to sixty-eight. We're a tight-knit group. We may joke about our grandfather's dismay at our failure to learn Greek or Latin, but when one of my cousins proposed that we organise Emek's memoirs and other documents, we worked together despite disparate lives and schedules until each of his children and grandchildren had a copy of the final bound volume.

My grandfather died in his Jerusalem apartment at the age of eighty-nine, following a series of strokes. By then he had seven grandchildren, one of whom was a captain in the Israeli navy he'd envisioned as a young man in Kraków. The most severe of his strokes – the one that would jolt his life off its foundations and leave him dependent – felled him on his daily walk. He lay for an hour on the secluded garden path between cypress and mulberry and Jerusalem pine trees, waiting to be discovered. What thoughts or flashes of memory, I wonder, might have kept him company during those endless minutes before his family was summoned? Or perhaps, in that interval before the shouts and the ambulance, before the start of the gruelling therapeutic process of salvaging what was salvageable, he was relieved for just a little while of the burden of memory, as he lay looking up into the high, pale sky of his beloved Jerusalem.

Last spring, following a thread of research, I typed "Krynica" and "liceum" into my browser. But I could make no sense of the links that came up on my screen. I tried different search terms. Still, the modern building that appeared repeatedly on my screen bore no resemblance to the one I knew. A quick address and map check placed it approximately six minutes' drive away from the old hotel building.

I searched further, eventually landing on a page full of sentimental comments by alumni commemorating their former high school.

The former Liceum Ogólnokształcące had been demolished in 2007. My family had not been notified.

The demolition of the town's old high school is captured in a series of photos. Tumbled bricks, broken panes, workers traversing the roof; dark gaps where the first windows have been removed. A quarter of the building is gone. Then half. Through the widening gaps in the successive photos, the forested hill behind the hotel emerges, and the neighbouring buildings, and the banks of the Kryniczanka stream.

On the site of the former Hotel Kryniczanka now sits a large block of apartments fronted by a bus shelter. Opposite it, Google's street view shows a pharmacy and a bakery-confectionary. Nearby are a grocery, a bicycle repair shop. Units in the building are advertised online for use by vacationers: Apartamenty Sun & Snow Krynica, available for booking. Decor is modern. In one photo you can see the slopes of the Beskids above the dark vertical bars of the balcony railings. Guest reviews of the rental units are generally good, with the best of the scores – 9.0 out of 10 – given for "Location".

Pull back from street view, and the screen is quickly overtaken by forests and fields. Seen from the height of a satellite, the apartment block is a small cluster of roofs – a few pixels in the splay of streets that is Krynica-Zdrój, afloat in the larger green tapestry of the mountain region. From

Perhaps he was relieved for just a little while of the burden of memory, as he lay looking up into the high, pale sky of his beloved Jerusalem

this vantage there is no evidence of where the hotel once stood. All that persists is a set of grey rooftops; the thin brown shadow of the Kryniczanka stream running behind them; and this love letter.

You are not forgotten.

You open the lace curtain. Outside, the first greening of the willow twigs. A splash of sun on the foothills beyond. A fitful, raw wind. Downstairs, your younger sister is protesting that her Purim costume will make her look like a child. Your two older sisters remind her that she *is* a child.

You'll come to her defence later. Today is a day to practise gymnastics on a mat in the empty, echoing ballroom. Prop the ballroom doors open to admit the wind. Then escape through them, unseen. Pass beneath the balconies, your footsteps quiet. Pass the waft from the stables. Follow the stream back and back into the foothills, until the roads and chimneys and steeples look small, and dream about the future. ≣

The unforgetting
of Zuzanna Ginczanka

Eva Hoffman

Outside her native Poland, the name "Ginczanka" is almost entirely unknown. Indeed, even in Poland, she was virtually forgotten for long periods after World War II – until a recent, and still intermittent, revival of interest in her life and work.

And yet, in her own lifetime – cut cruelly short by the Holocaust when she was only twenty-seven years old – she was successful and appreciated, renowned for her highly original poetry as well as her personal charisma, and a lively participant in the fertile literary culture which thrived in interwar Poland, and which included poets and writers such as Czesław Miłosz (who went on to win the Nobel Prize in Literature in 1980), the experimental poet-painter known as Witkacy, and Tadeusz Borowski, who later wrote a devastating collection of stories called *This Way for the Gas, Ladies and Gentlemen*. There were also well-known women novelists such as Zofia Nałkowska, all attracting a large readership.

"Ginczanka" was the chosen nickname of Zuzanna Gincburg, born in 1917, probably in the then Russian city of Kiev, but brought as a baby by her parents to the town of Rivne, which today is in

Ukraine but, in that region of frequently changing borders, became part of Poland in the interwar period, and was known as Równe. Ginczanka's birth coincided with a momentous event for Poland – the regaining of independence after nearly 125 years of partitions and conquests by the three neighbouring empires of Russia, Austria and Prussia. Baby Zuzanna was of course entirely unaware of such developments, but they crucially affected the course of Jewish culture in the new nation-state. For the first time in centuries of multicultural relations, Jews became citizens, rather than a caste, with all the privileges as well as obligations that such status brings – a change which led to a great flowering of Jewish political and cultural activity.

Równe was a town of about 50,000 inhabitants, divided between a well-to-do district with cosmopolitan pretensions and impoverished sections living separate lives. There was also a division between Poles and Jews, who constituted more than half of the population and were responsible for most of the town's industrialised enterprises, as well as practising various professions and trades. On return from Russia, Zuzanna's parents rejoined her mother's elderly parents, who were both pharmacists and ran a large variety store, in which, aside from medical supplies, you could purchase anything from children's toys to movie tickets. Ginczanka's grandfather was ailing and died not long after, but her grandmother was to be an important influence – especially after Zuzanna's parents divorced and abandoned her shortly after returning to Równe. Her father, who had some acting aspirations, left first, eventually ending up in New York. Her mother soon remarried and also left, making her way with a new husband to the rather unusual destination of Pamplona. Neither maintained any contact with their daughter, and we don't really know how

Zuzanna, who hardly had a chance to get to know her parents, felt about this double betrayal – but after their departure, she was largely brought up by her grandmother Chaja, a forceful and interesting personality.

Chaja apparently ran the pharmacy with great efficiency, and although she explicitly defined herself as "secular", her identity was forthrightly Jewish. In a period of extensive Jewish philanthropy, she helped poor Jewish orphans and old people, gave jobs to needy young women, and was active in supporting a Jewish orphanage and other charitable societies. She would not have thought of herself as a feminist, but she must surely have influenced the future poet's sense – so apparent in her writing – of female autonomy and power. At the same time, it may be evidence of Chaja's easygoing tolerance that at Christmas she placed her very pretty granddaughter behind the shop's window, dressed as an angel – a declaration that customers of all faiths were welcome.

She was being trained to be a proper – and properly acculturated – young lady of her time

Zuzanna started composing verses when she was just three or four years old, sometimes writing school exercises of some length in verse. In addition, under her grandmother's supervision, she had piano lessons, learned drawing and took private lessons in French from one "Madame Sauvage". In other words, she was being trained to be a proper – and properly acculturated – young lady of her time. Her accomplishments are evidence of the high level of education prevailing in the Polish borderlands in the early twentieth century, and the young age at which children often began secondary school. Zuzanna, who early on assumed the pseudonym "Ginczanka", entered one after third grade, making a crucial choice of a Polish-language school. In this multicultural region there were also schools that conducted classes in Yiddish, Ukrainian or Russian – the less favoured language of the former oppressor. Ginczanka's choice, however, had nothing to do with national allegiances, but rather with her affinity and deep feeling for the Polish language, so powerfully evident throughout her writing and sometimes stated explicitly: "My speech is for me my country," she declared in a poem called "Conjugation".

Ginczanka's more public literary career began in high school, with a student initiative to launch a magazine called *School Echoes*, which not only published its own students' work, but also encouraged contributions from those at other schools in Równe and its vicinity, in the various languages adopted there. Once the magazine got started, the editors apparently favoured prose over poetry, and Ginczanka, in an act of playful protest, wrote a plea titled "In Defence of Poets: An Appeal to the Editors", in what might be called rhyming prose. "It is my soul which has to write in the defence of all good verse and call with all its tiny might your harsh judgement to reverse," the budding poet wrote, signing herself "Sonny Girl" – one of the many pseudonyms and nicknames she assumed, seemingly as a form of verbal amusement.

Even at the age of fourteen, Ginczanka hungered after poetry; and her poems clearly showed that the hunger was accompanied by a rare talent. Here's a verse from one of the earliest, called "Holiday Feast" (Ginczanka's presence in English is minimal – there is still no English volume of her collected works – although small selections of poems have been translated, including this one, by Marek Kaźmierski):

In a dish of blackest glass, darker than a starless night,
A banana flavoured moon lies there yellow, fat and ripe.
July sprinkles starry light all around the waning moon,
As if stars were made of sugar in the cosmos' shiny spoon.

Translating poetry from Polish into English is exceptionally difficult, since Polish rhymes easily, while English does not – and Ginczanka, from the beginning, used rhymes and off-rhymes, as well as interesting rhythmic variations in her poems. Still, the love of nature and the synesthetic metaphors of "Holiday Feast" come through in the English version – and are an early signature of her style. How a fourteen-year-old girl achieved the boldness of imagination and expression necessary for this is one of the mysteries of talent; it was clear, even at her young age, that poetry was her calling – a vocation she followed unswervingly throughout her short life.

When uninterested, she was rebellious enough to fail mathematics in seventh grade and have to repeat the year. Her resistance to externally imposed discipline and her fearless independence of thought and spirit were also to characterise her poetic perceptions – and her actions – as she grew into adulthood.

Ginczanka's imagination was highly individual, but it was also fed by a breadth of reading and an awareness of the wider world, evident even in her early writing – for example, a cycle of poems titled "Chinese Fairytales about La-Lita", written when she was turning sixteen and based loosely on translations of Lafcadio Hearn's fairytales from English. The cycle follows an artificial girl's search for a real heart and humanity, and is again marked by Ginczanka's originality and rich expressiveness. At around the same time, her great childhood friend Blumka Fradis cited passages from the work of Katherine Mansfield. Clearly, the young women of Równe were reading international as well as Polish literature. The poet Jan Śpiewak, who visited Ginczanka when he was already a noted literary figure, remembers that she was, even in her teens, sophisticated – in her conversation, her self-confidence as well as her poetry – beyond all his expectations.

Ginczanka won her first literary distinction in 1933, when she submitted a poem ("Song About an Adventure") to a competition sponsored by a serious journal called *Literary News*. One of the judges was Julian Tuwim, the leading poet of interwar Poland, who was himself Jewish, and who became Ginczanka's sponsor and supporter. In a sense, this was Ginczanka's entry into Poland's wider literary culture, in which Tuwim was a presiding presence, and it is interesting to note that quite a few editors of *Literary News* were Jewish. Indeed, the flourishing of a specifically Jewish press was a phenomenon of the period in Poland, with around 130 newspapers of various political persuasions published in Polish, Yiddish and Hebrew.

Ginczanka followed her successful debut by submitting another poem, "Grammar", to *Literary News* under the pseudonym "Sana". "Adjectives stretch like cats, and like cats are made for petting," is a line from the long poem, which attributes various qualities to different parts of speech. Language, for her, was alive and sensual – something to relish, mould and play with; although the serious purpose of that play was to reflect reality, in all its manifestations.

But it was human, and especially female, sensuality that was one of Ginczanka's recurring preoccupations in her adolescent poems, and whose expressions and conflicts she registered with great candour. In "Rebellion of Fifteen-Year-Olds", she writes:

> Our legs are no longer gangly
> our shoulder blades don't stick out
> In the night, my thoughts astound me
> when the moonlight finds me out –
>
> … How hard during springtime mornings
> to still the blood in our chests,
> when mothers, frowning and fawning,
> want to keep us trapped in their nests.

Recent responses to Ginczanka's poetry often apply postmodern feminist theory to her work, but this seems to me somewhat misconceived. Ginczanka was clearly feminist by temperament and cast of mind, but this wasn't reflected in any explicit ideology or set of convictions. Indeed, in a period of intense Jewish activism and mixed-gender youth groups – Bundist, Zionist and sponsored by the religious Aguda party – she seemed (like so many poets) to eschew explicit ideological commitments. Her belief, I think, was in the power of poetry to clarify the world for us – and who knows, perhaps to make something happen.

Her poetry, however, often shows marked awareness of what today we would call class distinctions. In a startling poem called "Sheer Chance", written when she was sixteen, Ginczanka describes an encounter between herself and a woman whose condition speaks of very different circumstances:

> The thing is, my life is quite charming:
> Spacious home, creature comforts, sheer fun
> I've no idea what it means to be starving
> To be freezing (my nights rise with the sun) …
>
> She is all of sixteen years old.
> Gonorrhoea has mangled her flesh …
>
> All I know is that she has a child,
> Lost four fingers in an accident, or more,
> Her tradition a trade full of pride:
> Like mother and grandma
> To be a whore.

This is startlingly bold, as well as self-aware. But Ginczanka's emotional and thematic range was enormous. She could be a wickedly perceptive observer of more conventional women's lives, as in a poem called "Home", written in several voices:

married couple:
They run a convenience store (flour, sugar, pepper, butter).
His lips set hard – her looks no longer matter.
By midnight he is counting, on all he is able
To offer while she stares at their still silent cradle.

girl:
Words can be silent – silences can sing –
A vase holds a bunch of freshly severed things.
There are screaming senses and loving adored.
Bed linen. Night stand. A lampshade. All bored.

Ginczanka's biographer, Izolda Kiec, stresses her perennial sense of loneliness, which she attributes to Zuzanna's early abandonment by her parents; indeed, although she was pursued by various men, her relationships with them were always fraught, and may have never reached mutual fulfilment. But there are also portraits of powerful women in her poetry – as in "Joyful Mythology", whose narrator is startlingly compared to Atlas, carrying her own happiness – and sunlit space – on her shoulders. Elsewhere, Ginczanka strikes one of her main thematic notes, by presenting women – and indeed all humans – as part of the natural world, made of the same substance and inseparable from it. In "Fisherwoman", the narrator is in dialogue with the sea, as with a kindred element; in another poem, the protagonist speaks to a birch tree as her sister. In Ginczanka's poetry, there is nothing more natural than sensuality, and nothing more sensual than nature. And, as her poetry develops, her vision of the natural world expands, both in space and time – as in a poem called "Process":

... Cretaceous,

Jurassic,

Triassic,

Soil layered along certain rings –

Miocene assaults in majesty, conquering all things.

... At first there was heaven and earth

And fawns in the nest of the herd.

But then, the current changes.

Thus flesh

In the end

Became word.

The intensity and beauty of Ginczanka's metaphoric language are elements of her originality; her precocious development as a poet seemed to be entirely self-propelled. For a while, however, she belonged to a group of poets – the rest of whom were probably all men – who wanted to get away from the Polish version of romanticism by emphasising regional poetry of town and country – for some of whom she was a kind of muse, sometimes referred to as "Sulamit" (the Polish version of Shulamit, the beloved in *Song of Songs*), in tribute to her Middle Eastern beauty.

Ginczanka herself was fascinated by *Song of Songs* and wrote two poems titled "Canticum Canticorum" ("Song of Songs"), in which Shulamit and Solomon sing their love for one another. Although Ginczanka declared herself to be "pantheistic" and non-religious in several of her poems, she clearly knew the Old Testament well. But her mature poetry also contains references to the classical traditions of Greece and Rome, as well as to ancient

Israeli history, as in a narrative poem called "Son of the Stars", about the Bar Kokhba rebellion.

Given the expansiveness and breadth of Ginczanka's vision, her "tiny little town", as she describes Równe in one of her poems, may have come to seem confining. In 1935, when she was still in her teens, she moved to Warsaw, the country's cultural hub. One-third of its population was Jewish, and it was the centre of a thriving, multilingual Jewish culture. Warsaw was where the newly acculturated Jews tended to live, including writers, book publishers, filmmakers, recording artists and theatre actors. There were literary groups for writers who chose Hebrew, Yiddish or Polish as their language of expression, and which included novelists and poets whose names became famous throughout Poland, and sometimes the wider world – Bruno Schulz and Isaac Bashevis Singer among them. It is astounding that five of the most famous

She was also beautiful, in a way that fascinated many people and, in the end, did not serve her well

Polish poets in the interwar period were Jewish, including Alexander Wat, a modernist poet who had my favourite answer to whether he was Polish or Jewish: "I am Polish-Polish and Jewish-Jewish," he said, a formulation Ginczanka might well have applied to herself, expressing a deeply internalised bi-cultural identity. There was Jan Brzechwa, author of charming children's poems, and the most famous of them all – Julian Tuwim, whose poems for children we still memorised when I attended elementary school in post-war Poland. Tuwim was also known as the founder of several cabarets – a form of entertainment that survived World War II, functioning underground in post-war Poland. And there were cafés where writers congregated, sometimes reading their work to each other before it was published.

Ginczanka may have come to Warsaw with Tuwim's encouragement; his fondness of her and support of her work was important both to her literary successes and the tenor of her Warsaw life. In 1935, she entered the University of Warsaw, studying pedagogy at the Department of Humanities. But probably more important for her was her entry into the Skamander group of poets, led by Tuwim and considered the apex of Warsaw's literary life. The pecking order among such groups was clearly delineated, and everyone understood that Skamander was the top: the enchanted circle which all aspiring writers wanted to get into, but very rarely did. The conversations among them were lively, often playful, and at the same time professionally serious. When Tuwim telephoned Ginczanka, he would announce, "Zuzanna, this is one of the elders calling!" He also sometimes joked that she was both "dark and light beer" – referring to the different colours of her eyes (one was green, one was blue). Ginczanka herself emphasised the difference in a surviving self-portrait – which, incidentally, suggests that her ability as a graphic artist was also considerable. So was her talent for sharp satire, which she began to exercise in contributions to a Skamander publication called *Szpilki* (literally "Pins", although that doesn't quite convey the word's connotation of biting humour). She was admired not only by Tuwim, but by other Skamander personalities: Witold Gombrowicz, the experimental novelist and playwright who specialised in an intellectual mode of perverse irony, and who attained international fame from his post-war exile in Argentina; Kazimierz Brandys, an essayist and film writer whose renown spanned the pre- and post-war period; Józef Wittlin, who continued to write essays and novels in Polish from his post-war exile in New York; and yet others.

In 1936, a collection of Ginczanka's poems was published under the title *Of Centaurs* – her only book to come out in her lifetime. It was a stunning, much noted debut; Jan Śpiewak, who first met her in Równe, wrote, "She doesn't give up on anything, on melody, intonation, metaphor, urgent rhythms." Here are some fragments from the title poem:

I profess the dignified harmony of a masculine torso and head
To a stallion body and its slim legs wed
– to cool female cheeks
And napes of rotund mares…

… Their passion focused and wise
And their wisdom smoldering rapt
I found in a harmony dignified
and I alloyed them in waist and heart.

Ginczanka's poetry is marked by a desire for unity: of nature and human nature, of mind and passion, of word and world; she probably would have endorsed Virginia Woolf's idea that the imagination is androgynous.

During her Warsaw years, she continued to work hard, writing poetry and several radio programmes. But she also had enormous joie de vivre. The parties she gave at her rented flat were attended by many distinguished personalities, and we know from a few extant photographs that she attended the then popular dance clubs – sometimes in slightly risqué but elegant outfits. She was also beautiful, in a way that fascinated many people and, in the end, did not serve her well. Her friends and admirers noted her interesting eyes, and she was dark-skinned – a feature that enhanced her "exotic" beauty, but also marked her as distinctly Jewish.

*

Then, in the middle 1930s, the atmosphere in Poland began to change. In 1935, Józef Piłsudski – the de facto leader of the nation, well disposed towards ethnic minorities – died, and was in effect replaced by Roman Dmowski, the powerful head of the National Democratic Party, who wanted to make Poland ethnically "pure", and sanctioned boycotts of Jewish businesses. At the same time, the threat from Germany was becoming more menacing.

Ginczanka was clearly aware of these changes, and although she continued to attend lectures at university – where rising antisemitism sometimes resulted in assaults on students – she asked a male companion, tall and not to be attacked with impunity – to accompany her. She continued to eschew simple political positions, but some of her poetry clearly referred to current events. In "May, 1939", she writes:

> At times, hope in me rises,
> At others, I fear what's in store.
> Life is too full of surprises –
> What's coming? Be it love or war?

For her, it may have been both. The summer of 1939 – the fraught time before the cataclysm – found Ginczanka in Równe, but when the Germans invaded Poland in September, she fled to Lvov – a formerly Polish city now in the Ukraine, but then in the Soviet Union. So did many others, including large numbers of cultural and literary figures, many of them Jewish, who thought Lvov would provide a refuge from Nazism. For a while, it did, but it came with some unpalatable conditions attached. The writers gathered there were required to join the Soviet Writers' Union – and, in effect, to pledge allegiance to Stalin. They were also required to work for the regime; Ginczanka, who knew all three languages of the region, was employed as a translator.

Early in 1940, she married a man sixteen years her senior – possibly in the hope of being protected by his communist and non-Jewish credentials. She was in fact, perhaps for the first time, in a relationship of reciprocal love, with a young graphic designer, Janusz Woźniakowski, an arrangement apparently known by all parties. In 1941, however, the Molotov–Ribbentrop Pact, which supposedly guaranteed peace between the USSR and Germany, broke down, and Nazism arrived in Lvov.

The immediate consequence of the invasion was a terrible pogrom, in which Ukrainian inhabitants of the city eagerly participated. Ginczanka found a hiding place in a large building where an apartment had been allocated to her and several of her Równe friends by the Soviet authorities – and which turned out to be fraught with danger. The concierge of the building, named Chominowa, was viciously antisemitic. During Nazi inspections, she readily pointed out the hiding places of its Jewish inhabitants. Ginczanka's husband "legitimated" himself by showing his work permit. Others were caught, but Ginczanka managed to escape, perhaps not only from the building, but also from the police station – and she went on to write her most famous poem, "Non Omnis Moriar" ("Not All of Me Will Die"), a statement – even as she was facing deadly danger – of defiant rage:

> Non omnis moriar – my proud estate,
> of table linen fields and wardrobes staunch
> like fortresses, with precious bedclothes, sheets,
> bright dresses – all remain behind me now …

... And as I did not leave here any heir
You, Chomin's wife, the snitch's daring wife,
Volksdeutscher's mother, swift informant, please
Allow your hand to dig up Jewish things.

In a post-war trial of Chominowa (Chomin's wife) conducted by the Polish government, the poem was used as evidence – perhaps the only such instance in legal history – and Chominowa was sentenced to four years in prison.

The poem was, in a sense, Ginczanka's last will and testament. After the Nazi occupation, her husband decided it was time to leave Lvov, and they made their way to Kraków, where she went into hiding again. Her steps from then on are difficult to trace, but in one of her hiding places, she was helped by Jewish and non-Jewish people, some of whom belonged to groups trying to rescue Jewish children and adults by various means. There were fewer such people in Poland than the informers who gave Jews away but the risks they were taking were great – helping Jewish people in Nazi-occupied Poland was punishable by death – and they too need to be remembered and honoured.

During her Kraków hiding, Ginczanka was in a very reduced state, frightened and nervous, refusing to go out on the street or to travel to what might have been a safer place. Eventually, she was discovered or informed on, and taken to an infamous prison, where she was treated with particular cruelty. In an act of malignant intuition, the Nazi guards dragged her to interrogations by her hair – her beautiful black hair, which she particularly wanted to protect. She never confessed to being Jewish, but her friend Blumka Fradis, who was imprisoned with her, caved in, sealing both their fates. Probably in 1944, Ginczanka was transported to another prison, where she was killed – apparently walking to her execution with great dignity.

Ginczanka was murdered, in that most horrifying of catastrophes; but her poetry – which was as much a part of her living self as her body and mind – was saved by a friend, who spirited her manuscripts out of her Warsaw apartment shortly after she left it. Her last prophecy has been fulfilled: not all of her has died. In her poetry, she is a living presence; she speaks to us with an immediacy and eloquence that increases our sense of what was lost – and makes us grateful for what remains. ≡

Iran's revolution, the Jews and the televised debate

Lior Sternfeld

The 1979 Iranian revolution, which was supported by roughly 90 per cent of the country's population, has been described as the most popular revolution of the twentieth century. No wonder, then, that many of Iran's minority communities participated in it, including Iranian Jews, who supported an "Iranian" revolution, long before it turned "Islamic". They envisioned a republic that would eliminate the dictatorship and the corruption with which the Shah's regime was identified. The Jewish community aided and protected protesters and, while still in the euphoric early stages of the revolution, was even represented in the committee charged with drafting the new constitution after the removal of the Shah in January 1979.

In the first months of 1979, Iran experienced political and social chaos. Though it may be difficult to appreciate today, there was no inevitable trajectory leading to the establishment of the Islamic Republic. For example, shortly after Ayatollah Khomeini, the leader of the revolution, returned to Iran from his exile in France, he said that women would be required to wear hijabs. On 8 March 1979, International Women's Day, a million Iranian men and women took to the streets to protest his decision. Following this resounding response, Khomeini announced that hijabs would be recommended, not required.

After the revolution, Iranian Jews had more to fear than other communities. But it was also a time of great hope. In the pages of the Jewish press in Iran, the community's leaders debated whether to ask the incoming government to eliminate the seat in the Majlis (parliament) for the recognised religious minorities – Jews, Armenians, Assyrians and Zoroastrians. This seat had been granted in the 1906 Iranian Constitution, but in the new Iranian republic, they thought, Jews and other minorities would be able to get elected as part of the national lists; hence there was no need for a reserved seat.

But these debates and public protests about the country's future happened simultaneously with mass trials and speedy executions for the loyal servants of the old regime and those seen as enemies of the new regime.

One of the victims of these trials was Hajj Habib Elghanian, a former leader of the Jewish community, well-known philanthropist and the owner of Plasco, a leading firm in the plastics industry. (The high-rise Plasco building adorned Tehran's skyline until 2017, when it collapsed in a fire.) On 8 May 1979, Elghanian was arrested and put on trial. He was accused of spying for Israel, spreading corruption on earth, befriending God's enemies and waging war against God and his messenger, Khomeini. The trial lasted twenty minutes. The next day he was executed. His death shocked the Jewish community. Shortly after, a delegation of the Jewish leadership travelled to Qom to meet with the Ayatollah and seek assurances about its safety. Weeks earlier, the PLO had received the keys to the former Israeli embassy building. The worrying trend was that the Iranian public had started to conflate Judaism with Zionism. At the end of the meeting, Khomeini issued a religious ruling proclaiming that the Zionists are not Jews, that Iranian Jews are Iranians, and that their place is in Iran, as part of the new society.

Harun Yeshayaee, a prominent leader of the Jewish community in that period, recalled in his recently published memoir that, after the execution of Habib Elghanian, Iranian radio and television played their part in disseminating anti-Jewish propaganda. The Association of Jewish Iranian Intellectuals, the de facto leadership of the community, urgently attempted to counter these vile trends. The association had some connections with prominent leaders of the revolutionary government and suggested that a roundtable debate be aired on national television about Jews, Judaism and Zionism. The main national TV network, Shabakeh-ye Avval (Channel 1), agreed to host it.

The network decided on three televised debates. The main guests would be Aziz Daneshrad, a long-time Jewish left-wing activist and a member of the constitution drafting committee; Rabbi David Shofet, a well-known religious leader for Iranian Jewry and the son of the Hakham Yedidia Shofet, the chief rabbi of Iran at the time; and Dr Hossein Abutorabiyan, a prominent journalist and intellectual who had written extensively on Iranian politics and Palestinian issues. Other speakers were also invited. The three debates would be broadcast during prime time on consecutive Fridays, an Iranian weekend day off, which assured sky-high ratings.

The first broadcast took place on Friday, 22 June 1979, and considered the participation of religious minorities in the revolutionary movement. On this topic, the Jewish community had a lot to work with: during the violent anti-Shah demonstrations, the Jewish hospital in Tehran was known for treating wounded protestors and sheltering them from the notorious SAVAK (the brutal secret police). The hospital worked closely with Ayatollah Sayyed Mahmoud Taleqani – Khomeini's right hand in Iran prior to his return in February 1979.

The second debate came a week later and focused on Zionism (the third debate would focus on Zionism and imperialism). In those days, just mentioning the term Zionism was enough to cause havoc. Yet, astonishingly, a civilised – if intense – debate took place. The conversation started with Rabbi Shofet clarifying the difference between Judaism and Zionism. He explained that the word Zion came from the mountain in south-east Jerusalem, and that it is sacred for Jews because of the location of the holy temple. Furthermore, Shofet talked about the scrolls of Ezra and Nehemia, the Babylonian exile and the universal message of the return to Zion and global redemption, and that Jerusalem does not belong to Jews alone but to the entirety of humanity, and should be celebrated as such.

Daneshrad discussed the concept of *vatan* (Farsi for "homeland"), describing it as the place where a person is born; where their ancestors were born; where they live; where the local culture is their own; and where one wants to die and be buried. For him, he said, this place was Iran. He talked of the political Zionist movement, locating its roots in Europe. The cause of political Zionism, according to Daneshrad, was European nationalism and antisemitism. The failure to include Jews in the national projects of Europe led to the pogroms that in turn led the Jews to imagine their future using the same nation-building tools that the Europeans had crafted for themselves. Zionism required Jews from all over the world to come to Eretz Yisrael/Palestine and eventually establish a state there.

Daneshrad added that Zionism would have to transform into a model of sharing the land with the Palestinians (following a referendum; this is also the official stance of the Islamic Republic of Iran).

I have been unable to find the footage of this roundtable debate. However, I have spoken to a few interviewees who recalled watching it when it was broadcast. I could not find many references in the general Iranian newspapers, but it was covered by the Iranian Jewish press (especially in *Tamuz*, the official newspaper of the Association of the Jewish Iranian Intellectuals), and was discussed in some memoirs of former prominent figures in the community. One scene, of which I heard multiple versions, all along similar lines, stands out as a reflection of the undercurrents in Iranian society, the Jewish-Iranian community and beyond.

The host, so the story goes, asked Rabbi Shofet if it is true that "all the Jews are Zionists". This question alone could suck all the air from any room in Iran in 1979. Rabbi Shofet hesitated for a moment, then replied: "Jerusalem, Zion, for me, is like Mecca for you. Jerusalem is the place to which I make pilgrimage, a place I address my prayers to. If this is what you may call Zionist, then I am a Zionist, and all the Jews are Zionists!" Another version adds a brilliant sentence at the end, drawing on the average Iranian's intense animosity to Saudi Arabia, which, then as now, exceeds even animosity to Israel: "You pray to Mecca, right?" Rabbi Shofet apparently asked. "Does it make you a Saudi loyal?" ▤

Community

The Jews of Provence

Benjamin Ramm

In November 1940, Henri Dreyfus's sixteen-year tenure as mayor of the Provençal town of Carpentras came to an abrupt end. A month earlier, the Pétain regime at Vichy had passed a law barring members of the "Jewish race" from holding office. Dreyfus – the nephew of Alfred, whose ordeal helped define the Third Republic – was arrested in 1943, after the German invasion of the region, and deported to Drancy. He narrowly avoided being sent to Auschwitz, where his brother René perished, along with three extended family members. When the war ended, Henri returned to Carpentras, and was re-elected overwhelmingly to serve a final term as mayor.

This story is a small but significant chapter in the history of Carpentras, home to the oldest active Jewish community in Western Europe and the second oldest on the continent (after Prague). Jews first arrived in Provence over two thousand years ago, landing at Marseille in the company of Greek merchants. The region has been both a cultural innovator and a neglected backwater; once part of the Holy Roman Empire, it became a seat of papal power before being subsumed into the French state. Throughout its many incarnations, the Jews have remained – resolute, at times flourishing, often suffering, and always nurturing a distinct cultural legacy.

My visit to Carpentras was timed to coincide with the much-anticipated regional elections in June 2021. Part of the city's complicated Jewish story is the recent revival of far-right support in this area of Provence. Journalists in Paris had been writing breathlessly about the prospect of "the south" embracing "fascism", and I was curious to understand why – and to what extent – far-right sentiment had re-emerged.

In Jewish tradition, "Provence" is a cultural rather than an administrative demarcation. It incorporates the influence of neighbouring Occitanie, particularly the eastern towns of Narbonne, Montpellier and Lunel – founded in the first century by Jews from Jericho – as well as cities with a strong Catalan identity, such as Perpignan. (The flag of Provence still features the red-and-yellow *senyera* banner of Catalunya.)

A decisive chapter in the story of Carpentras begins in 1306, when King Philippe "le Bel" expelled the Jews from France. Prior to this, most Jews had lived comfortable lives. Their religious education required them to read and write, and many became doctors, teachers, bookbinders or bankers, as well as landowners, farmers and even winemakers. During the medieval period – when the secular troubadour poets were in their ascendency – Provence became a celebrated centre for Torah study.

The rabbis of this region, known as *Hachmei Provence*, blended practices from the Sephardim to the south-west and the Ashkenazi Tosafists to the north-east. Their prayer rite – a distinctive liturgy in Provençal, a dialect of Occitan – closely resembled the Italian style. This was particularly evident in Nice (*Nizza*), where the Jewish community had its own dialect and an affiliation with Piedmont.

In response to Philippe's order of expulsion, Pope Clement V offered Provence's Jews residence in his papal enclave known as Comtat-Venaissin, of which Carpentras was made the capital in 1320. Jewish life soon coalesced around the communities of Avignon, L'Isle-sur-la-Sorgue, Cavaillon and Carpentras – together known as "Le petit Jerusalem" (an analogy with the four quarters of the Old City).

Construction on the synagogue of Carpentras – the oldest in France – started in 1342, and for almost a century Jews fared well: the inhabitants of the Comtat did not pay taxes and were not subject to military service. But their status was never guaranteed; some of the Avignon popes were favourable, protecting Jews against reprisals during the plague, while others were punitive, even resorting to expulsion. By 1461, when Provence was ruled by "Good King" René, the "Pope's Jews" of the Comtat had been forced into a ghetto.

While the conditions in Carpentras were not as severe as elsewhere – for most of the year, Jews were allowed "out" during the day – the restrictions made life extremely claustrophobic. With more than a thousand Jews in a space of roughly 1500 square metres, the 168 houses of the ghetto were cramped, unstable highrises. During my visit, community elder Alain Freund gave me a tour of the synagogue and described how, five hundred years ago, "they had to build up eight, nine, ten stories". Forbidden from owning property, Jews were obliged to wear a yellow symbol, and by the sixteenth century their professions were restricted to secondhand trading and usury.

There was even a prohibition on windows that looked onto the town. Forced inward, this community soon developed its own dialect, Judéo-Comtadin, of the language Shuadit (or Judéo-Occitan) spoken in Provence. The isolation of the Comtat, especially after the expulsion of the Jews from France in 1498, ensured that the four congregations shared an idiosyncratic character, and a literature of their own: *piyyutim*, or liturgical poems, that combined Hebrew and Provençal.

Life in the ghetto revolved around the elegantly ornamented synagogue, which attended to every aspect of community life, from the *mikvah* to the *shechita*. The site had two bakeries: one for challah (with an oven forge that could fit up to 2000 loaves) and another for unleavened bread at Passover. The synagogue was twice enlarged during the eighteenth century, in the Provençal baroque style, to reflect the growing community – a tenth of the town's population.

During the French Revolution, members of the Jacobin Club, whose campaigns against organised religion were particularly virulent in the papal states, used the synagogue as a meeting house. In 1791, the National Assembly annexed the Comtat (which now comprises the *département* of Vaucluse), and Jews became French citizens – "emancipated", as a public plaque proudly states, with equal rights for the very first time. When the Bourbon monarchy was restored briefly, from 1814 to 1830, Jews were forced back into the ghetto.

After the revolution, the Provençal rite was replaced by the Portuguese Sephardic liturgy, which is still used by the community today. Emancipation led to a degree of assimilation, and use of Judéo-Provençal declined. Mr Freund tells me that one elderly lady still speaks a smattering of the dialect, but the last fluent speaker was Armand Lunel, a prominent writer who died in 1977. In 1926, Lunel won the inaugural Prix Renaudot for his novel *Nicolo-Peccavi, or The Dreyfus Affair in Carpentras*.

Lunel wrote extensively about the community, including *Jerusalem to Carpentras* (1937); the libretto for an opera, *Esther of Carpentras* (1938), based on Shuadit folklore; and a study of Provençal Jewry, *Jews of the Languedoc, Provence and the French Papal States* (1975). He was well known in the region, and married the daughter of architect Aaron Messiah, who designed the Villa Ephrussi de Rothschild on the Côte d'Azur.

The decline of Judéo-Comtadin raises some tricky questions about the nature of Jewish identity in a secular age. How do we mourn the loss of a language that emerged as a consequence of ghettoisation? Every dialect is a unique way of seeing and being in the world, and its disappearance is a kind of obliteration of memory. But in recent years, particularly among Ashkenazi activists uncomfortable with Zionism, there has been a tendency to fetishise the ghetto – which ignores why so many Jews left as soon as they could. The corollary of these questions is: what does it mean to be Jewish in an environment in which the threat of extinction is not self-defining?

This was not something the Jews of Provence had the luxury of finding out for themselves. Although only on the border of Vichy control, Jews in the Vaucluse faced severe restrictions to their liberty and livelihood for the first time since the revolution. Between 1941 and 1942, le Camp des Milles, outside Aix-en-Provence in Bouches-du-Rhône, was used as a transit camp for 2000 Jews who were deported to Auschwitz, via Drancy; a museum at the site commemorates their journey. A considerable number of French Jews – up to 240,000 – took refuge in and around Nice, after Italy occupied the region in November 1942. Jews were safer here than in Vichy France: the Italians refused to cooperate with the Nazis in rounding up Jews in this occupied zone, and actively prevented deportations. But the Italian armistice with the Allies prompted the Germans to invade all of Provence, on 8 September 1943, after which they formed specialised units to hunt down Jews. Within five months, 5000 were caught and deported to Auschwitz.

At the train station in Sorgues, twinned with Châteauneuf-du-Pape, a memorial records the deportation of August 1944, when 403 Jews – who had been forced on a death march via the picturesque vineyards – were loaded onto cattle tracks destined for Dachau. At Sorgues, as in Marseille, there was local resistance, including the sabotage of train lines, which facilitated the escape of 200 of the original 720 deportees.

After the war, the community of Carpentras underwent a change in composition. As North African states gained independence from France, immigration from the Maghreb increased, and Carpentras welcomed Jews from Morocco, Tunisia, Libya and Algeria (*pieds-noirs*). The majority of the present community is from this region, including Mr Freund's Tunisian wife, Katia, who is the public face of the Association for the Enhancement of the Jewish Heritage of Carpentras. Alain is the sole Ashkenazi member of the congregation.

In recent years, the town has earned an unenviable political reputation: in 2012, Marine Le Pen's niece, Marion Maréchal, became the youngest citizen ever elected to the French parliament, aged twenty-two, when she won Vaucluse's third constituency – which includes the southern portion of Carpentras. (As if to highlight the notoriety, the previous youngest MP was Louis Antoine de Saint-Just, zealous executor of the Terror, elected in 1791, aged twenty-four.)

In 2015, Maréchal led the far right to victory in the first round of regional elections in Provence–Alpes–Côte d'Azur, which took place a month after terrorist attacks killed 130 people in Paris. Maréchal lost in the decisive second round to a Republican, and Le Pen failed to win a single region, but there was speculation that 2021 might be different.

Four weeks before the election, the Republican incumbent, Renaud Muselier, was photographed with Mr Freund in the synagogue, to celebrate a recent renovation. Alain did not demur from acknowledging the significance of the visit, and he emphasised the congregation's "excellent" interfaith relations: he meets regularly with his Catholic counterpart in the Gothic cathedral next door, and with an imam from the growing Muslim community, whose presence is notable during the town's famous Friday market.

The political views of Jewish *pieds-noirs* are often caricatured as reactionary, yet Mr Freund says there is little support for the far right among members of the synagogue. Le Pen's candidate, Thierry Mariani, a former government minister under Nicolas Sarkozy, grew up in Vaucluse, and it was assumed he would find popular favour in the region. In fact, he lost to Muselier in the second round by a considerable margin on a low turnout, winning only a handful of constituencies – one of which, narrowly, was Carpentras.

*

In the Jewish cemetery of Carpentras, established in the fourteenth century with annual dues paid to the Pope (consisting of six pounds of spice, pepper and ginger, or the silver equivalent), there lie the tombs of the most established families of the Comtat. These include Milhaud (notable for the twentieth-century composer Darius); Crémieux (famed for the nineteenth-century politician Adolphe, who granted French citizenship to Algerian Jews); and Vidal-Naquet – ancestors of the eminent intellectual Pierre (1930–2006), whose anti-fascism was motivated by knowledge of his father's torture at the hands of the Nazis. In 1990, neo-Nazis dug up and mutilated the body of a recently buried member of the synagogue – one of a wave of graveyard desecrations that gained widespread media attention.

The community today gathers on high holy days, and for a once-monthly Shabbat service, in the majestic prayer hall on the first floor of the synagogue. Alain opens the ark to reveal, behind a partition, two dozen *Sifrai Torah*, beautifully adorned and carefully maintained. Opposite is a spiral pulpit, in the style of a baroque church, with a view of the most curious feature: Elijah's armchair – a small, gilded, red velvet throne, for the "prophet of children" to witness the circumcision of baby boys.

On a sultry Friday evening in June, congregants milled around the synagogue square. The Shabbat service I attended was informal and convivial, led by Dr Meyer Benzekrit, a charismatic Ladino-speaking dentist of Turkish origin. The minyan seemed like a large family, with each member, in their own unassuming way, keeping alive a flame that ought to have been extinguished long ago, but which – despite everything – still burns after seven centuries. ▤

Reviews

The heretical hope of Jacob Frank

Benjamin Balint

The Books of Jacob
Olga Tokarczuk
Translated by Jennifer Croft
Riverhead Books (US)/ Fitzcarraldo Editions (UK)/
Text Publishing (Australia)

In her latest book – the first to appear in English since she won the 2018 Nobel Prize in Literature – Polish novelist Olga Tokarczuk traces the picaresque adventures of the messianic pretender Jacob Frank.

Heinrich Graetz, the nineteenth century's leading Jewish historian, reviled Frank as "one of the worst, slyest, and most deceitful villains of the eighteenth century". Gershom Scholem, the twentieth century's most influential Jewish historian, called Frank "one of the most frightening phenomena in the whole of Jewish history … a truly corrupt and degenerate individual … a figure of tremendous if satanic power". In 1916, the 28-year-old writer S.Y. Agnon expressed undisguised aversion: "[He] and his gang were not a limb of the body of Israel; rather, they were a [pathological] excrescence. Praise and thanks to our doctors, who cut it off in time, before it took root in the body!"

What makes Jacob Frank so disquieting a figure? *The Books of Jacob* – published in Polish in 2014 and now appearing in Jennifer Croft's beautiful, lithe translation – is woven on the weft of that question.

On the surface, the novel, populated by a large roster of real-life *dramatis personae*, hews close to historical fact. ("I write fiction," Tokarczuk has said, "but it is never pure fabrication.") The time is the second half of the eighteenth century. The setting is the borderlands of the Polish-Lithuanian Commonwealth – then the largest Catholic country in Europe and home to the largest Jewish community in the world. Feudalism is giving way to the era of the Enlightenment, with its emancipatory aspirations, its syncretism, its hopes of revolution.

Jacob Frank was born in 1726 in Podolia, in the south-eastern part of Poland, grew up in Wallachia (a region of Romania under Ottoman rule) and restlessly flitted as a salesman through Czernowitz, Smyrna, Bucharest, Sofia and Constantinople. According to his biographer Paweł Maciejko, Frank lived as an eternal outsider, "an Ashkenazi among the Sephardim, a Sephardi among the Ashkenazim, a Pole among the Turks, a Turk among the Poles, an unlearned boor among the sages, a sage among the simpletons".

In 1754, Frank travelled with his wife, Hana, to Salonica, "filled at this time with every sort of mage and miracle worker", Tokarczuk writes, with "some self-proclaimed Messiah or dark sorcerer offering instruction on every street corner". There he first experienced the spasms of *ruach ha'kodesh* (the holy spirit), founded his own house of study and persuaded his first followers – paupers, vagrants, itinerant peddlers, miscellaneous mystics and "Christian ragamuffins" – that "the curtains between this and that world had been rent".

The next year, Frank and his hangers-on crossed the Dniester River from Ottoman territory into the Polish Commonwealth, where he began to practise bizarre behaviour, or "strange deeds" (*ma'asim zarim*). In January 1756, for instance, at an inn in a town called Lanckoronie, Frank led a ceremony later described by the great Talmudic scholar Rabbi Jacob Emden:

> And they took the wife of the local rabbi (who also belonged to the sect), a woman beautiful but lacking discretion, they undressed her naked and placed the Crown of the Torah on her head, sat her under the canopy like a bride, and danced a dance around her ... and in dance they fell upon her kissing her, and called her "*mezuzah*," as if they were kissing a *mezuzah*.

Besides holding ecstatic seances, Frank publicly violated Shabbat, pronounced the name of God (*shem ha'meforash*) and boasted of sitting on a Torah scroll, "my ass naked". Speaking in riddles and parables, he taught that the old dogmas and decrees – notions of sin especially – had been rendered obsolete. Frank and his followers rejected the Torah and the Talmud in favour of the esoterica of Kabbalah. To dismantle the old order and build the new, they felt that they must "wipe the Mosaic Tablets of their false commandments that keep them imprisoned like animals in cages". Frank proposed instead "purification through transgression".

The leaders of Polish Jewry rejected this false faith and excommunicated its leader. Tokarczuk has Rabbi Hayyim Cohen Rapaport of Lwów pronounce the Frankists "worse than the Pharaoh, than Goliath, the Philistines, Nebuchadnezzar, Haman, Titus ..." The crisis culminated in two public disputations between the traditional Talmudists and the Frankists (or contra-Talmudists). In the first,

held in 1757, the Polish consistory court found the Frankists inno-
cent of heresy, and ordered copies of the Talmud burned throughout
Podolia. In the second disputation, convened in the Lwów cathedral in 1759, Frankists made cynical use of blood libels and of the
sensational "revelations" by the most famous eighteenth-century
Jewish convert to Catholicism, Jan Serafinowicz, who falsely
claimed to have twice participated in ritual murders of Christian
children. "When a people turns against itself," says Rapaport in
despair, "it means the sin of Israel is great."

Though initially regarding themselves as a new type of Jew, the
Frankists were soon seized by a hope: "That once they are baptized,
they will cease to be Jews, at least as far as anyone can tell. They
will become people – Christians." Most of those who wished to
flee their own foreignness believed that just as Sabbatai Tzvi had
crossed over to Islam a century earlier, Frank (whom they called
"the Lord") would achieve salvation through Christianity. They
called this "walking to Esau", after the Biblical figure identified
with Rome and Christianity. This led to the largest voluntary apos-
tasy in Jewish history: Frank and thousands of his followers were
baptised in 1759.

Rabbi Emden urged the Catholic leaders in Poland to reject
the Frankists:

> In truth, even according to the Gospels no Jew is permitted
> to abandon his Torah ... The Nazarene and his apostles did
> not come to abrogate the Torah, heaven forbid, for as it says
> in Matthew that the Nazarene says: "Do not think that I have
> come to abolish the Torah; I have not come but to fulfill it. Even
> if heaven and earth will be abolished, nevertheless even one let-
> ter or jot from the Torah will not be abolished but will abide."

With varying degrees of whispered suspicion, Poles regarded the converts as orphans or superstitious savages to be taken into the church's bosom, or (as Tokarczuk has one priest say) as "so many dogs shooed from a yard who will seek shelter under any old roof at all". The Poles wondered, too, about the unpredictable Frank, a man possessed of such great powers of persuasion: Was he a holy fool? A debauched psychopath? A boorish libertine? Or a miserable Messiah who descended to the darkest depths in order to ascend to the highest spheres?

Not long after the mass conversion, Frank was denounced to church authorities, found guilty of proclaiming himself the Messiah, and confined for the next thirteen years in the fortress-like Jasna Góra Monastery in Częstochowa, home to the Black Madonna icon. Frank came to believe that the divine presence was captive in that venerated image of the Virgin Mary. "I was put here," he said, "because this is where the *Shekhinah* is imprisoned, on this new Mount Zion."

Liberated by Russian troops in 1772 and issued with passports by the three states partitioning Poland (Russia, Prussia and Austria), Frank fled with his retinue into exile: first to Brünn, Moravia (now Brno in the Czech Republic), and later to a disused castle in Offenbach, Germany. In his declining years, Baron von Franck, as he was by then known, was plagued by disappointment despite his life of opulent luxury. "Who among you have ever truly believed in me? You are all fools. I've been struggling over you in vain. You've learned nothing."

On Frank's death in 1791, bells rang out from all the churches of Offenbach. He left his followers with a question that teetered between religion and nihilism: if the Messiah had already come, why did history remain fundamentally unaltered and unredeemed?

Gershom Scholem contended that the Frankists helped ease Jews out of the ghetto and into nineteenth-century liberalism. "When the flame of their faith finally flickered out," he writes in his essay "Redemption Through Sin,"

they soon reappeared as leaders of Reform Judaism, secular intellectuals, or simply complete and indifferent sceptics … Their "mad visions" behind them, they turned their energies and hidden desires for a more positive life to assimilation and the Haskalah, two forces that accomplished without paradoxes, indeed without religion at all, what they, the members of "the accursed sect," had earnestly striven for in a stormy contention with truth, carried on in the half-light of a faith pregnant with paradoxes.

To this day, Poles debate the Frankist ancestry of famous figures, including the poet Adam Mickiewicz and the composer Frédéric Chopin. In her 2007 novel *Flights*, Tokarczuk told of a nineteenth-century traveller who smuggled Chopin's heart back to Poland under her skirt. In *The Books of Jacob*, she recounts the afterlife of Frank's skull:

Many years later, under unknown circumstances, it made its way to Berlin, where it underwent detailed measurement and research and was labelled a prime example of Jewish racial inferiority. After the Second World War, it vanished without a trace – either it was destroyed in the turmoil and chaos of war, crumbling to dust, or else it is still lying around somewhere in the underground storage facility of some museum.

All of the preceding is fact. Aware that narrative, including history, is necessarily imprecise, however, Tokarczuk tells the story of Frank by ingeniously interweaving narrators both reliable and unreliable – and it is here that *The Books of Jacob* spreads its majestic wings and lifts from fact into fiction. The novel's most reliable narrator in is the all-seeing and ever-present Yente, Frank's grandmother, whose gaze moves effortlessly through space and time. In the opening scene, she swallows an amulet, a paper bearing the Hebrew word for "waiting" (*hamtana*), and becomes permanently suspended between this world and the hereafter. Just as the *Shekhinah* is trapped in matter, so is Yente tethered by the dissolved word.

Tokarczuk's most unreliable narrator is Nahman, a former student of the Baal Shem Tov who imperceptibly shifts from being Frank's master to his friend, then his ardent disciple. "I remember that I got goosebumps at the sight of him, I felt my body tremble, and I experienced a love greater than I had ever felt for anyone before." Ostensibly writing *The Life of His Holiness Sabbatai Tzvi*, Nahman in fact secretly jots down Frank's doings and dicta. "Nahman's stories are not always to be believed," Tokarczuk cautions, "even less so when he writes them down … He has a propensity for exaggeration. He detects signs in everything."

Nahman, like Tokarczuk, experiments with three narrative modes. First, the objective: "I believe that what I describe really happened, and that it happened that way once and for all." He comes to see this way as "false". Second, the subjective: "I focus on my own experiences … Then everything is more about me than it is about Jacob, his words and acts are made to pass through the sieve of my tangled vanity." Nahman dismisses this perspective as "pathetic". Finally, he learns to "surrender to the guidance of my own Hand, my own Head, Voices, the Ghosts of the Dead, God, the Great Virgin, Letters, Sefirot".

In the end, Nahman surrenders to the knowledge that, like Yente, who remains neither dead nor alive, Frank and his flock are neither Jewish nor non-Jewish. "We are foreigners' foreigners," says Nahman, "Jews' Jews." But that is perhaps not such a terrible fate. "There is something wonderful in being a stranger," Nahman tells himself, "in being foreign, something to be relished … Only foreigners can truly understand the way things work."

In each of her books, Tokarczuk approaches a subject from the periphery, as though she too were a foreigner. *The Books of Jacob*, her masterpiece, was published in Polish with an elaborate title (in homage to the title of a volume by Father Benedykt Chmielowski, the first Polish encyclopaedist): *The Books of Jacob, or the Great Journey across Seven Frontiers, Five Languages and Three Great Religions, Not Counting Several Minor Ones: Narrated by the Dead, Their Story Being Completed by the Author According to the Method of Conjecture, Expressed in Several Books, but also Assisted by the Imagination, Which Is Humanity's Greatest Natural Gift: A Record for the Wise, A Reflection for My Compatriots, An Instruction for Laypersons, Entertainment for Melancholics*. The title, like the vast novel itself, points towards a religiously and linguistically plural Polish past. Its frontier-crossing characters speak a polyphony of Yiddish, Turkish, Polish and German (none of them with any precision) and inhabit multiple identities (none of them clear-cut).

When the novel won Poland's highest literary award, the Nike, Tokarczuk said in a television interview, "We have come up with this history of Poland as an open, tolerant country, as a country uncontaminated by any issues with its minorities. Yet we committed horrendous acts as colonisers, as a national majority that suppressed the minority, as slave-owners and as the murderers of Jews." (The ancestors of those murderers figure in the novel; Tokarczuk has a Catholic clergyman say: "It's an odd thing that the Tatars, the Aryans, and the Hussites were all expelled, and yet somehow no one thinks to get rid of the Jews, although they are the ones bleeding us dry. Abroad they even have a saying about us: Polonia est paradisus Judaeorum.")

The interview occasioned a wave of hate mail and death threats, as though readers sensed that beneath the surface, the novel carries a subtle but subversive commentary on both present-day Polish homogeneity and the entanglements of the Polish-Jewish past in a country that became for its Jews not a paradise but an inferno.

According to Tokarczuk, messianism became the most paradoxical of those entanglements. "For people brought up in Polish culture," she has said, "messianism is important – our Romantic literature was soaked with it." Yet because messianism is at root a Jewish idea, Polish culture rests on an impossibility: "that you can take a Jewish idea to build Polish identity and exclude Jewishness", as Tokarczuk put it in a 2018 interview for *PEN Transmissions*, the magazine of English PEN.

Identity is fluid and imprecise, and its imprecision disquiets those who seek purity. One of the novel's ancillary characters writes to Father Chmielowski: "Maybe the whole art of writing, my dear friend, is the perfection of imprecise forms." In *The Books of Jacob*, Olga Tokarczuk has mastered that art. ▤

The archaeology of Cynthia Ozick

Tali Lavi

Antiquities
Cynthia Ozick
Knopf (US)/ Weidenfeld & Nicholson (UK)

In his recent book, *Three Rings: A Tale of Exile, Narrative and Fate* (2020), writer and classicist, cultural critic and translator Daniel Mendelsohn writes about the historian-philosopher Erich Auerbach, a Berlin-born émigré who found refuge in Istanbul during the war. It was in that city that he produced *Mimesis*, a foundational text of comparative literature. Mendelsohn notes that Auerbach later recognised "that it was, in fact, his exile, his eastward wandering across borders and nationalities and continents, that made possible his great study of *Weltliteratur* ... much of which, legend has it, he had to write from memory of the various texts".

I was reminded of Auerbach's achievement when I read Cynthia Ozick's new novel, *Antiquities*. Ozick is one of the few people alive today who might accomplish such a staggering feat – who possesses so many of these *Weltliteratur* references at her fingertips. Auerbach of course experienced a radically different historical reality, exiled from his home, country and language as he escaped the murderous Nazi regime. But Ozick shares a strangely similar sensibility of exile, along with a capacious mind that allows her to wander through multiple overlapping histories and stories.

For readers who know Ozick's name but are not intimate with her life and work, there may be some bewilderment at this identification of her as a writer of exile. She was, after all, born in the fabled *Goldene Medina,* in New York City in 1928, and grew up in the Bronx. Yet, as she declared in a talk given in Israel in 1970 (later published as "Towards a New Yiddish"): "Diaspora, *c'est moi.*"

Ozick was born into a family of Russian immigrants with recent embodied memories of bloody pogroms. As a young child she was sent to a boy's *cheder,* where she not only received religious instruction, but also learned Yiddish and developed what would be a lifelong love of Jewish culture. While she grew up in a loving household with a bookish pharmacist father, a mother "aflame with ambition, emotion, struggle", and an older brother who nourished her reading habit, antisemitism was a rupturing force. In her childhood, Ozick encountered taunts of "Christ killer" and had stones thrown at her as she ran past the local church. She was old enough by the late 1930s to be aware of the unfolding conflagration in Europe. The Shoah – what was lost and what remained – is a major preoccupation in her work, veering between being a shadowy and a palpable presence. Other recurring fascinations include the power of language – the exhilaration of its potential and the weight of its responsibility; ancient and recent memory; the lives of émigrés; and the spilling over of ardour into fanaticism.

Ozick has garnered a deserved reputation as one of America's finest minds, a dazzling *maven* of multiple forms: the short story, criticism and the novel. Handsome paperbacks have recently been reissued of her uncompromising Shoah classic *The Shawl* (1980), its successor "Rosa" (1983), *The Bear Boy,* a masterful Victorian-style novel examining money and ideology (also known as *Heir to the Glimmering World*, 2004) and her *Collected Stories* (2006).

Antiquities, a deceptively slim novel, conceals multiple strata. The novel takes us into the head of eighty-year-old Lloyd Wilkinson Petrie, who lives in Temple House, a home for a dwindling group of ageing Trustees and former students of the defunct boys' prep school Temple Academy, which the building once housed.

The year is 1949. Lloyd is a Waspy echo of Yiddish poet Hershel Edelshtein, the protagonist of Ozick's 1969 short story "Envy; Or Yiddish in America". Both men are obsessive egotists. Edelshtein is "moored" to fellow poet Baumzweig through their "agreed hatred for the man they called *der chazer* [the pig]", another Yiddish poet called Yankel Ostrover, who is translated and feted while they live in obscurity. Lloyd, in contrast, is a retired lawyer who admits that he is "no philosopher, my leanings are wholly pragmatic". But like Edelshtein he is vindictive and vituperative, intolerant of the happiness of the old men who read "incomprehensible poetry" to each other under the stately maples in the grounds of Temple House.

Ozick captured something in Edelshtein, with all his insufferability, his old-world accent and his angst, the way he lives in and for a vanishing language. The same language in which my own grandmother told jokes that verged on ribald. I would listen to her moan about her ageing body or repeatedly inform us, in case we had momentarily forgotten, that she and her sister had once been fabled beauties in the pre-war rural Carpathia where they had grown up. Like Rosa in *The Shawl*, my grandmother lived through the horror of the murder of her toddler daughter, whose qualities she would intone in Yiddish. Edelshtein knows what is at stake, what we risk forgetting with the disappearance of this singular language, the original vessel that simultaneously held and spoke of the depths and flights of European Jewish tragedy and joy. Ozick encapsulates this in English, brilliantly evoking the American Jewish experience during the twentieth-century era of migration and flux.

Lloyd barely inspires pity, though his rarefied world is also being upended: Temple House is being sold and its inhabitants turfed out. The memoir commissioned by the few remaining Trustees – *no more than ten pages!* – reveals deep internal fault lines.

At Temple House, the Trustees live "in considerable comfort in the identical site of … [their] early misery", with lovely gardens, mullioned windows and chandeliers. The fastidious narrator's self-containment has remained intact even after the death of his "dearest Peg", his secretary of many years and also his lover; her gravestone bears his careful words, "Margaret Gertrude Stimmer, A Companion Valorous and Pure". But now, as he writes his memoir, Lloyd finds this solitary but composed existence disturbed. Suddenly, "all is maundering, all is higgledy-piggledy". He finds himself in "a state of suffering of the soul" induced by the wounds of the past being picked and the subsequent flood of unsettling memories.

Among his possessions, Lloyd has held on to some artefacts brought back from Egypt by his father, spoils from when Petrie senior briefly abandoned his new wife and a golden future in the family law firm to join a dig led by his archaeologist cousin. They are miniature "oddities" or "arcana": "clay lamps, jugs … amulets", "grotesque figurines" with "bulbous female contours", a jar in the shape of a stork. Are these artefacts remnants of ancient civilisations or are they passable reproductions? Probably a mix of both. As a child Lloyd had hidden them away at the privileged but spartan Temple Academy, named for its founding family and inhabited by the offspring of wealthy parents, "unwanted half-orphans" like himself. He hints that he was subject to taunts. As he now beholds these objects, which sit on a shelf above his desk, the spectre of a long-dead, elusive father obsessed with the ancient world is raised. The ageing Lloyd is overwhelmed by memories of his father silently gazing at his collection, housed in a glass cabinet in his study, and panicked by the notion that his "father harbored somewhere in his ribs an untamed creature".

Alongside these artefacts lies his father's "small private notebook crackling with grains of sand trapped in its worn and brittle spine", the residue of sand a lingering reminder of his father's frustrated dreams. There is something of E.M. Forster here; a passage into the heart of desire in exotic climes. The notebook is prosaic – it "reads as if copied from a Baedeker". Ozick, who deftly fuses civilisations, myths and mystical splendour, is more akin to Herodotus and his *Histories* than she is to Baedeker. "Cousin William" is Sir William Matthew Flinders Petrie, the real-life British archaeologist and Egyptologist, whose methods are still employed in modern archaeology and who conducted pioneering excavations in Palestine. Ozick is herself a literary archaeologist, unearthing lost and strange histories, layered over time; there's the hint of an affinity to Flinders Petrie, who desired to "search in the Holy Land for all those famed yet lost and buried Biblical cities".

(A further intriguing layer of interest: *Antiquities* includes an acknowledgement of the archaeologists Rachel Hallote and Alexander Joffe, "for entry into the world" of Flinders Petrie. Hallote, a professor of history, is Ozick's daughter, Joffe her son-in-law. Curiosity about what lies beneath has been inherited. Clearly Ozick does not share Lloyd Petrie's despair at his own son, who "shuns the ancestral", antiquities and the stories of his patrician Protestant family for the parallel universe of mid-century Hollywood.)

At the heart of *Antiquities* is the curious subject of Lloyd's memoir, Ben-Zion Elefantin. His first name, meaning "Son of Zion", sounds "preposterous" to the Christian boys around him, though it is a normal enough Hebrew name. It is his surname which is odd. Petrie recalls Ben-Zion as a "grotesquerie". He is utterly unlike the other Jewish boys who have gained admittance to the Temple Academy, and wholly unlikeable. He is shockingly other. He eats only bread, milk and hard-boiled eggs (we are to understand he keeps kosher), and has "astoundingly red" hair, "deeper and denser and more otherworldly" than an Irish red. Perhaps it is the legacy of King David, the reader wonders, though the theory is later rejected. He may wear a kippah; there are signs of *payot*. Lloyd hears the boy's "incantations" morning and evening across the corridor. On visiting his room, he spies an "eerie contraption" (tefillin), and a "very old" book with illegible letters. Ben-Zion has his own antiquities, but to him they are invested with meaning. A game of chess between the two friendless boys, both of whom are trying to avoid school sport, initiates a tentative comradeship. The fallout is swift; Lloyd has crossed the unforgiveable line, and "I too became persona non grata".

In the early twentieth century, when Lloyd and Ben-Zion were schoolboys, antisemitism was alive and kicking at Temple Academy, where even the Jewish boys who were physically indistinguishable from their peers and might "pass" were not able to do so, despite the enlightened openness of the school's master, Reverend Greenhill. Lloyd may not have actually said the word "Hebe", but he confesses to having thought it. He remembers the frequent shattering of the school's chapel windows by locals who, because of its name, thought it was a Jewish institution. As absurd as this is, it's hard to laugh; the broken glass slyly prefigures Kristallnacht. Among the overt references to antisemitism – Dreyfus, Shylock – Ozick threads through more subtle iterations. As an old man, Lloyd still occasionally sees a former schoolmate who became a wealthy judge. "That is how these people are, their overflowing sentimentalism," he muses, in what might be read as a bitter reference to his son's defection to Hollywood. "Their motion picture style of exaggerated feeling."

Ben-Zion was not merely a Jew, a foreigner, a strange beckoning force. His voice, which Lloyd describes as "mysteriously archaic … uncannily ancestral", hinted at something beyond. The narrator confesses, "I hardly know my own meaning as I tell this." As in the work of Henry James (one of Ozick's seminal influences, who has a cameo role in *Antiquities* – his portrait sits in the Academy vault), truths are obscured in her fiction; veils are pervasive; mystery is integral. Reading Ozick's fiction is to experience a sensation bordering on pain, linked to the realisation that we may never completely understand elements of her intricately constructed worlds. Seers, often female, manifest themselves. The brilliant scientist Elsa Mitwisser in *The Bear Boy* is one: a German refugee who refuses to relinquish her former home and whom the American narrator, Rose Meadows, perceives to be "a sibyl", "alert to the subterranean calamities of the world". In *Foreign Bodies*, Lili, a survivor of the Shoah who works with refugees in post-war Paris, plays a similar role. These women are haunting and haunted figures. Initially, we suspect them to be spectres until we realise that they not only are repositories for hidden knowledge, but also possess an agency not apparent in their male companions.

One of the mysteries embedded in *Antiquities* is the origin story that twelve-year-old Ben-Zion Elefantin long ago divulged to ten-year-old Lloyd. And now, after seven decades, Lloyd has become his amanuensis. Following the strange declaration, "I am Elefantin," a story emerges, delivered with a prophet's zeal. The narrator describes Ben-Zion's "utterances" as "akin to a burning bush". The story goes thus: his ancestors had taken part in the Exodus from Egypt but, "unyieldingly faithful to Moshe", they did not worship the golden calf. Instead, they returned to the Egyptian island of Elephantine, built a temple and strictly adhered to the traditions of the Bible. They never made it to Jerusalem and their practice was literalist, devoid of rabbinic interpretation. Their fate was to "live on as apparitions", outcasts from formal Judaism.

(I do my own digging, though I suspect Sir Flinders Petrie would not approve of my methods. I employ Google and discover that the Jews of Elephantine did indeed exist. Hundreds of Aramaic papyri attesting to their history were discovered on the island at the turn of the twentieth century.)

This is not the first time Ozick has explored alternative Jewish histories. In *The Bear Boy*, Professor Mitwisser is obsessed by the Karaites, a sect of Jews who, like the Jews of Elephantine Island, rejected rabbinical Judaism and strictly followed the written Torah. Rose, Mitwisser's assistant, learns that the Karaites "are dissidents; therefore they are haters. But they are also lovers, and what they love is purity, and what they hate is impurity." In a *New Yorker* interview early in 2021, following the publication of a new short story, Ozick admitted, "I have always been drawn to the idea of the fanatic, the zealot, the proselytizer, the Johnny One-Note, the deceiver, the false explainer – the enemy of the ordinary." She once branded the founders of New Criticism – a mid-twentieth-century critical movement that insisted literary meaning is to be found solely in the text – Karaites.

Early in her career, Ozick claimed that the storyteller is an idolator. In an interview published in the *Paris Review* in 1987, she retracted that earlier assertion: "One *cannot* be a monotheist without putting the imagination under the greatest pressure of all. To imagine the unimaginable is the highest use of the imagination … You simply cannot be a Jew if you repudiate the imagination." Her passion for literature borders on fanaticism, "that glorious but perilous worm", as she writes in *Critics, Monsters, Fanatics and Other Literary Essays* (2016). Acutely aware of the weight of words and how their misuse corrupts history, Ozick enjoys teasing out their possibilities and experimenting with their magical properties, but she does not countenance laziness or folly. She has deconstructed the unwitting misuse of the term "Kafkaesque" ("Transcending the Kafkaesque", from the same collection), penned a letter to the editor of the *New York Times* in the form of a poetic riposte to Lionel Shriver's review of *Antiquities* and, more seriously, addressed the public legacy of Anne Frank, in a 1997 *New Yorker* essay. In the *Paris Review* interview, she describes herself at twenty-five, reading "eighteen hours a day, novels, philosophy, criticism, poetry, Jewish history, Gibbon … I read and read and it made me into some kind of monster. I'm still that monster." Some of her characters are versions of the obsessive young Ozick: Ben-Zion, Reverend Greenhill and Hedda in *Antiquities*; Rose and Professor Mitwisser in *The Bear Boy*; Lars in *The Messiah of Stockholm*, who believes himself to be the secret orphan of Bruno Schultz and for whom reading is his self; Julian in *Foreign Bodies*. Readers will revel in this recognition of reading as a boundless desire that might tip into the uncomfortable realm of obsession.

Antiquities, like some of Ozick's other novels, is replete with references to Jewish history. They move through the work as sinuously as the Nile along which Lloyd's father once journeyed, and beside which Ben-Zion's ancestors founded a home. Lloyd's tone is elegiac as he speaks of his losses and the collapse of this, his Temple. The Temple falls, one by one the trustees begin to die; it is the narrator's own *Book of Lamentations.* Freud, Heine and Buber are invoked, the first two by Hedda, a German Jewish refugee and the resident cook (her *Sachertorte* is scorned for being "absurdly irrelevant"), whom Lloyd disdains as "postwar flotsam and jetsam". Even Ben-Zion's reference to *Adam Bede* – he is an avid reader of the English classics – is a tacit reminder of George Eliot's philosemitism. This subtle accretion of layers and references is one of the many pleasures of the novel.

"Who will care for them as my father cared, and I after him? Who will be moved by their antiquity?" wonders Lloyd of his treasured artefacts. At least we, as readers, can take consolation from *Antiquities* and its place in Ozick's complex oeuvre; a trove of stories and objects that traverse the ancestral, religious, literary and personal. ▤

Correspondence

"The strange death and curious rebirth of the Israeli left" by Anshel Pfeffer

David Myers

I read with great interest Anshel Pfeffer's detailed analysis in "The strange death and curious rebirth of the Israeli left". I always learn from his reportage and writing. Very few journalists writing on Israel today can match his attention to historical detail, access to sources, and wit.

Pfeffer hinges the decline of the Israeli left on a mix of factors: ideological fatigue, institutional laziness, misguided emphases and abandonment of core Zionist commitments. Thirty years of Labour Party rule did indeed lead to ossification, both of ideas and structures, and an outsized sense of entitlement and privilege. It is important for those with a progressive/liberal/left bent to acknowledge failings frontally. It is also important to ask why, if the stunning victory by Menachem Begin known as *ha'mahapach* (the overturning) occurred in 1977, the left has remained enfeebled for so long.

Pfeffer homes in on the familiar charge of elitism, symbolised by the transformation of what was once a group of hardscrabble, anti-materialist kibbutz dwellers into cultural snobs who favour niche issues and the creature comforts of their Tel Aviv penthouses. There is certainly something to this, but it is essential to recognise other elements that are not mentioned in his article.

Let's begin with a long-term perspective on Israeli political history, which might profitably be divided into two phases: the first marked by the thirty-year rule of Labour until 1977, and the second by the reign of Likud, which has dominated the Israeli political landscape ever since. This latter period has been tumultuous; a courageous prime minister from Labour was assassinated by a fellow Jew, the unprecedented peace process with which he was synonymous rose and fell, and a violent uprising subsequently broke out that created wellsprings of doubt and uncertainty in Israelis. None of that redounded to the benefit of the left, in no small part because of the machinations of one Benjamin Netanyahu. He not only exploited Yitzhak Rabin's death to win a turn as prime minister in 1996, but used his second tour to erode the foundations of Israeli democracy in ways that targeted and disabled the left.

The end of the second phase of Israeli political history may be upon us. It has been a period, similar to the ending of the first phase, in which intellectual and institutional fatigue were amply present, along with a healthy dose of corruption. We may now be at the outset of a third phase, which Pfeffer begins to excavate, in which the categories of left and right are less relevant than a new pragmatism of which the current government is an example. The issue here is less about renewing the ideological tenets of Zionism than delivering practical and evenly distributed benefits to all, regardless of race, religion or gender.

In tracing the arc of this political history, it is helpful to take stock of another key development that was conterminous with the major realignment of 1977: the creation of a robust, grassroots civil society sector in Israel. In a certain sense, these two developments move in opposite directions: the first refers to a top-down process featuring political elites; the second to a bottom-up process that relies on grassroots actors working anonymously every day. The organisation of which I serve as president, the New Israel Fund (NIF), was established in 1979, urged into action by activists in Israel and abroad to attend to needs that were no longer being met by the social welfare policies of a Labour government. NIF has been a major presence in the bottom-up, civil society revolution in Israel, helping to birth and provide support to hundreds of other non-profit organisations devoted to the wellbeing of women, Mizrahim, Arabs, Ethiopians, Haredim, Russians and many more. At this level of activity, change comes every day, often in small victories, below the radar, in the form of a new clinic, newfound access to a public institution or the defence of previously suppressed rights. If you add up these triumphs, you get a coherent and effective theory of change.

So along with a sense of urgency and even despair regarding the state of liberalism – and mindful of the prospect that Israel may be entering a third phase in its political history – we must also recognise that meaningful change, often driven by the left, can and does come from the bottom up. This is cause for neither self-congratulation nor self-laceration, but rather for a long-term vision and commitment to fulfilling the ideal of a truly egalitarian society.

David Myers is the president of the New Israel Fund, and the Sady and Ludwig Kahn Professor of Jewish History at the University of California, Los Angeles.

Neil Rogachevsky

Why has the Israeli left been electorally impotent for a generation now – despite the participation of the two principal left parties – Labour and Meretz – in the current anti-Netanyahu governing coalition?

This is the question Anshel Pfeffer sets out to ask in his characteristically well-reported and astute essay. Pfeffer shows that Israeli leftists are not entirely beholden to illusions. They see what everyone else sees: a majority of the Israeli public still blames the parties of the left for the Oslo Accords – seen as a failure of both concept and execution – and the bloody Second Intifada (2001–2005) that followed, a national trauma of the order of the Yom Kippur War.

Various rebranding efforts have failed, as Pfeffer also shows. Perhaps this is because even when leftist leaders, such as current Labour leader Merav Michaeli, manage to maintain politic silence about immediate prospects for a two-state solution, they still fundamentally see their task in terms of "ending the occupation". One might argue that this is the necessary position to hold. But it's one that only interests a very narrow segment of the Israeli public. The left need not suddenly discover the potential virtues of annexation in order to be more relevant. Yet if it adapts what one could call the "consensus Israeli position" of maintaining the bad status quo while improving Israel's geopolitical situation and the economic prospects of Palestinians, the parties of the left may finally be able to draw level with the other parties in foreign affairs.

Pfeffer mentions that voters who formerly voted left now have other alternatives in the centre, and notes, correctly, that Israel has become more religious. But the transformation of Israel into a fairly conservative country is not addressed in the article nor sufficiently appreciated – by Israelis and foreigners alike. Benny Gantz's Hosen L'Yisrael and Yair Lapid's Yesh Atid are frequently referred to as parties of the centre. But by international standards, they look in many respects like parties of the centre-right. Just two examples can suffice here. In the election campaigns, Gantz criticized Netanyahu from the right – on the Palestinian question to some degree but especially on Iran. In a twist that might interest UK readers, Yair Lapid wrote the preface to the recent Hebrew translation of Roger Scruton's *How to Be a Conservative*.

The political dilemma facing the Israeli left is not dissimilar to the dilemma facing other left-wing parties in the Western world: how to balance the interests of often-young urbanites with woke politics and the bread-and-butter concerns of the traditional working classes who have often been on the losing end of neoliberal globalisation. The problem, however, is doubly difficult in Israel because the neoliberal turn in economics, which could in fact pose grave problems for Israel down the road, has been a boon for Israelis until now. Yes, the rent is too damn high. Yes, the roads are crowded. Yes, new infrastructure is needed. But a clear majority of Israelis are much richer and more economically secure than they were when the left was last relevant. Whatever their opinions of Benjamin Netanyahu, most Israelis have become addicted to the kind of political settlement that he managed. And, of course, a not insubstantial number of Israelis think he made the country economically stronger and more secure. The parties of the left will have to find a way to talk to this reality – or else hope a future crisis will redound to their benefit.

Neil Rogachevsky teaches Israel studies and the history of political thought at Yeshiva University, New York City.

Ori Yehudai

Anshel Pfeffer provides a rich and extensive account of the quandaries of what he calls the "Israeli left", focusing primarily on the Zionist centre-left and its political parties, Labour and Meretz, which struggle to reconcile the notion of a Jewish state with democratic and egalitarian values. The Labour movement dominated Zionist politics from the 1930s until 1977, returned to power for short yet significant periods in the 1990s, but more recently seemed on the verge of extinction. The smaller Meretz, to Labour's left, was founded in 1992, played a prominent role in the Labour-led government formed in that year under Yitzhak Rabin, but lately faced similar hardships to its bigger sister. Following the most recent elections, both parties returned to government, yet while in 1992 they won together fifty-six (out of 120) parliament seats, today they hold only thirteen.

As Pfeffer notes, this new reality created an identity crisis for the Zionist left – especially for Meretz, whose rallying cry has traditionally been opposition to the Israeli occupation of Palestinian territories and support for a two-state solution, and who now sits in a government dominated by right-wing parties abhorring those positions. While Labour and Meretz joined the coalition for the urgent task of ousting the corrupt and increasingly undemocratic Benjamin Netanyahu, their participation in the government might undermine the struggle against the occupation. Their leaders, in the meantime, focus on civil and social issues such as environmentalism, public health and transportation.

Identity crises are not new to the Zionist left. This is exemplified by the case of Ha'Shomer Ha'Tzair, a youth movement founded in Eastern Europe in the early twentieth century, which later created a kibbutz movement and a political party and became one of the pillars of Labour Zionism. In the 1920s, it adopted Marxist socialism, whose universalist values it could not reconcile with its particularistic Zionist ideology. It thus developed a "phases theory" giving precedence to Zionism over socialism. Movement members later debated their ideological loyalty to the Soviet Union amid revelations of the oppressive Soviet system. During the 1948 Arab–Israeli War, movement representatives in the government opposed harsh measures against the Palestinians, but after the war their kibbutzim gained lands of displaced Palestinians.

Those contradictions are perhaps inherent to Zionism generally – a movement of national liberation of an oppressed people which also had colonialist features and realised its mission through the dispossession of another people. But if in its heyday the Zionist left vacillated between conflicting ideological tendencies, today its dilemma is between adherence to ideology and loss of political influence: if Meretz forcefully resists Israeli policies towards the Palestinians, it will have to leave the government and become marginal again – and perhaps pave Netanyahu's way back to premiership.

Pfeffer writes that the left will remain "a bit player" until it finds new ideas. With no solution in sight to the Israeli–Palestinian conflict, the path for revival may be an alliance with Palestinian citizens of Israel. This will require an ideological compromise from a Zionist perspective, as the parties representing Palestinians in Israel generally reject the definition of Israel as a Jewish state. The flexibility needed for such an alliance may be found in the words of Palestinian Labour Knesset member Ibtisam Mara'ana. Although "Arab society doesn't believe in the [Israeli] left anymore", she says, she is not "responsible for" debates over the meaning of Zionism: "Everyone can define themselves however they like, as long as they don't marginalise me. I'm responsible for connections and there's no Israeli left without an Arab secular left." Such pragmatism – which also led Ra'am (the United Arab List) into the current coalition – may be the basis for Jewish–Arab partnership and a new life for the Israeli left.

Ori Yehudai is the Saul and Sonia Schottenstein Chair in Israel Studies and Assistant Professor of History at Ohio State University. He is the author of Leaving Zion: Jewish Emigration from Palestine and Israel after World War II.

Anshel Pfeffer responds

The political failure of the Israeli left to form a government is so old and entrenched that the multiple reasons for it have grown old as well. Everyone by now has their own pet theories, usually with a strong self-serving element.

I agree with David Myers that we need to take a long view of the left's political decline, bearing in mind that it has been taking place since 1977, when Likud first won an election. In the forty-five years since, Israel has had a Labour prime minister for only seven years. Even adding the three years of the Kadima government, Likud has been in power for more than three-quarters of this period.

Looking at Israel's second political era from a broader perspective, two observations jump out. First, the Oslo process began sixteen years after 1977, and its failure, in the bloodshed of the Second Intifada, ended eighteen years ago. Yes, the left's focus on the Israel–Palestine conflict is one of the main reasons for Oslo's decline. But there is a tendency to overemphasise it.

The second observation is that Benjamin Netanyahu became Likud leader the same year the Oslo process began and, in total, has led Likud for twenty-one years – less than half the period. Netanyahu without a doubt has done more than any other figure to toxify Israeli politics and taint the left as defeatists and even traitors, but he was working within an already deeply divided Israeli society. His expertise has been to exploit and deepen those divides. He didn't invent them.

Staying with Netanyahu for a moment, it's important also not to exaggerate his electoral success. In fact, under his leadership, Likud's share of the vote shrank. The average tally of seats won by Netanyahu's Likud is much smaller than that won by the party under the other three Likud leaders in this period.

Netanyahu's record-breaking longevity in power has been a result of his skill in building a resentful underdog coalition based on his ironclad alliance with the orthodox communities, which shifted in this era to the far right.

Another feature of this period has been the enduring success of many left-wing policies. The Oslo process may have foundered and the two-state solution seems unachievable, but it's wrong to focus just on that. In 1977, when Labour was still in power, Israel had full military control of the territories captured in 1967. Since then, Sinai has been returned to the Egyptians, the main Palestinian cities of the West Bank have been put under the control of the Palestinian Authority, Israeli troops have been withdrawn from the Gaza Strip and Israel has held various rounds of talks with the Syrians over the future of the Golan Heights (including twice under Netanyahu).

On the social level, there is much better integration of Arab-Israeli citizens and unprecedented openness towards the LGBTQ community, and the right to free healthcare and education, as well as to massively subsidised universities, remains as widely accepted in Israel as in the days of a socialist government.

As Myers points out, there have been hundreds of small but significant victories achieved by NGOs like the New Israel Fund on behalf of minority communities. In many aspects, Israel is a much more open and less conservative society today than it was during the three decades of Labour governments.

The left's failure, therefore, is a political one. In many ways, the left's agenda has prevailed, but the parties of the left have failed to translate that into votes.

I fundamentally disagree with Neil Rogachevsky's attempt to apply the framework of contemporary American politics to Israel. The Israeli centre-left is not "woke". In fact, one of the most fascinating experiences I had in working on my essay was discovering that most of my left-wing inter-viewees feel there is a widening gulf between them and their progressive contemporaries in America. And while the Israeli right – in particular the sections in thrall to Netanyahu – share many traits with Trump's supporters, especially the combination of religion and nationalism, their "conservatism" remains rooted in Israel's social-democratic traditions of universal public health and education services, comprehensive social benefits, including paid maternity leave, as well as easy access to abortion. It's true there are some fringe elements calling to dismantle the Israeli welfare state, but they are as marginal on the Israeli right as the young "woke" social-justice performers are on the Israeli left.

Israel isn't a social-democratic paradise and, if we're fully honest with ourselves, it wasn't one under Labour governments either. But, as the pollster Dahlia Scheindlin points out in my essay, on many issues, an overwhelming majority of Israelis hold what would be seen in America and most of the Western world as left-wing positions.

Israeli society has of course changed over the decades. It is more openly religious, and Mizrahi Israelis, who were marginalised under Labour's rule, have asserted themselves. The left's political leadership failed to adapt to these changes.

But if Likud's enduring success in the second phase of Israeli political history was built mainly on the realignment that saw the two main Jewish orthodox communities – the national-religious and the Haredim – ally firmly with the right, then the third phase, which Israel may be entering now, will see new realignments. As Ori Yehudai notes, the eagerness of pragmatic parts of the Arab-Israeli community to participate fully in Israeli political life as parties to government, and the increasing openness of parts of the Jewish majority (including on the right) to such partnerships, are an opportunity for the Israeli left – not just to change the electoral balance, but to reinvent itself as an ideological and political camp that can be a home for all parts of Israeli society.

Anshel Pfeffer is a senior correspondent for Haaretz *and Israel correspondent for* The Economist, *and the author of* Bibi: The Turbulent Life and Times of Benjamin Netanyahu.

Past issues

THE JEWISH QUARTERLY
May 2021

The return of history:
New populism, old hatreds

Simon Schama
Viral prejudice and the Jews

Mikolaj Grynberg
Poland's conflict with history

Holly Case
Viktor Orbán's Hungary

Deborah E. Lipstadt
White insurrections: Antisemitism in America

Isaiah Berlin
The Israel letters: Newly discovered correspondence

Hadley Freeman
on second-generation Holocaust memoirs

Benjamin Balint
on Paul Celan

plus Elena Ferrante, Ian Black, Robert Manne

"For a long time now, the authority of knowledge has been under siege from those who march under the banner of pure belief."
—Simon Schama

The Return of History: New Populism, Old Hatreds investigates rising global populism, and the forces propelling modern nativism and xenophobia.

THE JEWISH QUARTERLY
August 2021

The new Middle East:
Shifting allies, enemies and loyalties

Nir Baram
After Oslo: A farewell to peace

Lina Khatib
Pragmatism in the Middle East

Elie Podeh
Secret histories: Israel's road to normalisation

Deborah Levy
Too much past

Anne Sebba
The collection

plus Nancy Kobrin, Magda Teter and correspondence

"Traditional principles and allegiances have given way to realpolitik."
—Lina Khatib

The New Middle East: Shifting Allies, Enemies and Loyalties examines the dramatic changes unfolding in the region as new rivalries, blocs and partnerships are formed – based not on ideology but on pragmatism.

Past issues

THE JEWISH QUARTERLY

November 2021

The strange death and curious rebirth of the Israeli left

Anshel Pfeffer
On a new era in Israel

Richard J. Evans
The early days of a Nazi ideologue

Natalie Gryvnyak
Ukraine and its Jewish president

Raphael Zarum
The last rabbi: Jonathan Sacks and his legacy

Lauren Elkin
The personal journalism of Vivian Gornick

Barry Schwabsky
From Salome to Betty Boop

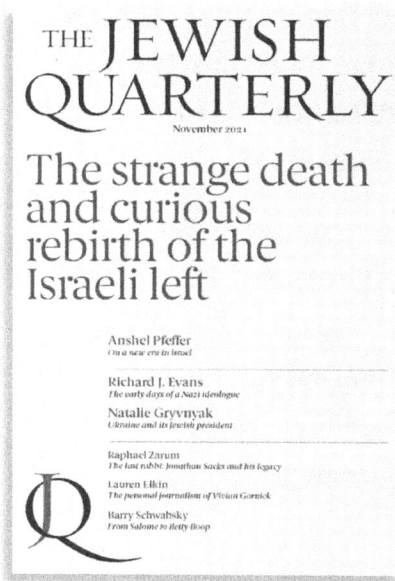

"The left has become the ideology that dare not speak its name."
—Anshel Pfeffer

In *The Strange Death and Curious Rebirth of the Israeli Left*, Anshel Pfeffer takes the pulse of Israel's left wing, examining its health and prospects and dissecting the country's complex post-Netanyahu political reality. He concludes that until it comes up with a new story to tell Israelis, the left will remain a bit player in the country it once built and ruled.

Add JQ244: *The Return of History* (May 2021), JQ245: *The New Middle East* (August 2021) and JQ246: *The Strange Death and Curious Rebirth of the Israeli Left* (November 2021) to your subscription when buying online.

Subscribe to The Jewish Quarterly and save.

Enjoy free delivery of The Jewish Quarterly to your door, digital access to every issue of The Jewish Quarterly for one year, and exclusive special offers.

Forthcoming issue:

JQ248: *After the Golden Age* (May 2022)

Never miss an issue.
Subscribe and save.

- 1 year* print and digital subscription (4 issues) £42 GBP | $56 USD
- 1 year* digital subscription (4 issues) £25 GBP | $32 USD

Subscribe now:
Visit **jewishquarterly.com/subscribe**
Email **subscribe@jewishquarterly.com**

Scan one of these QR codes with your mobile device camera app:

Subscribe in £GBP

Subscribe in $USD

PRICES INCLUDE POSTAGE AND HANDLING.
Prices and discounts current at the time of printing. We also offer subscriptions in AUD for subscribers from Australia, New Zealand and Asia, and for existing subscribers to Schwartz Media titles. See our website for more information. *Your subscription will automatically renew until you notify us to stop. We will send you a reminder notice prior to the end of your subscription period.